26 Miles

MY MARATHON

JAMAL BROWN

Keep Running...

ISBN: 9781092958707

Keep Running...

This book is dedicated to the-day-to-day people in the world who go unnoticed along with their thoughts and opinions. You are not alone.

I want to give a special shout out to Nipsey Hussle for vicariously instilling the Marathon philosophy and mindset in me. In addition, thanks for creating a blueprint and platform that I can use to maneuver through the loopholes in this wicked society.

Also, I want to give a special shout out to Shabazz the OG for the constant consistent "free game" he gives daily with no ulterior motive.

Last but not least, thanks to everyone I've encountered thus far through life that gave me advice and kept me sane on my marathon.

In most poverty-stricken areas across the world, we are given three options to escape life in the hood:

- Playing Sports
- Selling Drugs
- Becoming a Rapper

I CHOSE TO WRITE!!!

When the world turned its back on me,

I was up against a wall,

I had no foundation,

No friends and no family to catch my fall,

Running on empty,

With nothing left in me,

But doubt,

I picked up a pen,

And wrote my way out.

– Aloe Blacc

Keep Running...

This book contains poems, notes, and short stories that describe my thought processes at various points in my life which pertain to a host of different situations. Through the good times and the bad times, I survived to tell the tale. From my marathon to yours, pace yourself!

Table of Contents

Introduction

Would you rather be wise or knowledgeable? What is the difference between the two? Wisdom is evidence from experience. Knowledge is the accumulation of facts based on research, observation, and surveys. During my journey through life, I've either have seen it, done it, or heard about it. The experiences are recurring. Some come with different scenarios and perspectives. Nonetheless, the lesson is being taught over and over.

I live by the phrase "life is a marathon, not a sprint". Patience can be a superpower if you use it correctly. In the pages to follow, I will take you around the track of life on which I ran my miles. Our thoughts are universal, so you will find most of this content relatable. Put on your running shoes and pace me as we run through these pages!

Keep Running...

Every journey begins with a single step...

There comes a time in our lives where we feel forced to jump off the cliff in attempt to land face flat on an opportunity that will make our lives great like frosted flakes! We will never know until we jump.

This book is my leap of faith.

Even though I don't know what's on the other side, I must jump. It has to be better than surviving on this side.

Nothing beats a failure but a try.

KILL BROTHER BROWN

It's time to kill Brother Brown,
Kill that ego, and give the people the real Brother Brown,
It is no secret that you are indecisive,
You used to love everything, now you don't like shit,
Lately, I've noticed your energy has been off,
You have to fix it at all costs,
Everyone loves Jamal; they miss him,
Shit, I miss him too,
I've been looking for him,
I've looked everywhere,
In the mirror,
In the club,
In the classroom,
At the crap tables in the casino,
On vacations,
There is no reward for finding Brother Brown,
I can't afford to pay a prize fee,
If anyone sees him just let him know I am looking for him,
Thanks in advance.

-   Management

THE MARATHON

Life is a marathon,
Each lap around the track we become "wiser",
For some - "dumber";

Wisdom is evidence from experience,
We learn from our own mistakes,
and vicariously through the mistakes of others around us;

Life is not a straight line,
It is a full circle,
Each lap around the track or events revisited,
We see much deeper and clearer
as we pace ourselves through our personal journeys
to become unreasonably happy;

When we take full advantage of the coincidences that occur in our
lives, Only then, our lives will expand for the better in ways we have
never
imagined or fathomed,
Life is rough,
It's a race in itself;

Life is a marathon
Not a sprint,
Pace Yourself!

WORDS FROM THE WORLD

Many people vent to me daily. These are some of the stories.

HOW SWAY?

It's Payday, I wake up and rub my hands like Birdman. I check my paystub and see Uncle Sam hit me twice. Reality sets in and I am back hurting all over again. I am getting financially fucked into submission. They got me by the balls yawl and they are not just holding them, they squeezing my shits.

I'm paying so much money in taxes and child support, I myself can't eat. I can't afford an extra ranch sauce from the chicken spot. No money to take out this new chick I got. What the fuck am I working for? What is the point of working at all? The more I make the more they take. I try to stay happy, but the stress is written all over my face. Pockets bleeding from being financially raped. You don't care though. Free money is how you see it.

(To the child): It is not about me anymore. I know that I have to feed you. But, it is not just you. I have another two. They both look just like you. You all are my kids in the eyes of the world, but in mine sometimes I'm sorry to say I see you all as a bill. A goal I can't fulfill. It's hard for me but love outweighs all opponents. Still I climb.

Your mom ain't shit, she just wants to have everything on fleek. She gone taint your mind and tell you that I am out running the streets, chasing freaks, and that's why I am absent at night when it's time to tuck you in your sheets. Is this the reason you look at me funny on the 1 day I get to see you out of the week? There are three sides to a story though; her truth, my truth, and The Truth. When dealing with humans whomever taints the child's mind first will sway their thoughts away from the other parent. You will understand this later in life.

I admit I am so young and dumb, I thought buying you clothes here and there and posting a picture was taking care of you. I see by the way you fuck up them new Jordan's and Timbs, you can give two shits about clothes and shoes. You smile the hardest when you are naked running around in your purest form. It's the time spent in the physical form that matters. My presence is a present. Silly me. I'm learning though.

Keep Running...

I know my pride is diminishing the black family structure. I really want to be at the bus stop sending you off to school and picking you up. I want to read to you with your mom while we all cuddle on the living room couch. I want to be in the next room, so you can come sleep with me when you have nightmares. I want to be all the support you need. I am the only one stopping me from doing so. You will suffer greatly if I don't rid myself of this foolish pride.

I am selfish; I only want to get back with your mom when someone else wants her. As soon as it happens, I am quick to diminish her character and make her miserable without me. I don't want her though, I mean I do but I want to keep my hoes too. I told you I am selfish. To my kids: You will probably want to fight me when you all get old enough.

You all were not mistakes. I do not regret having you at all. I just wish the circumstances were different. I wish child support wasn't milking me on a weekly basis, and I got to know your mom as a friend instead of just chasing some ass. Only death can do us part. I live for my kids. I will make most of whatever time the judge allows me to see you all.

Close your ears when you hear your mom and I argue. We just have a difference in opinion. When she is losing the argument or situation she uses you as weaponry against me. I just have one question for her.

HOW THE FUCK CAN I SUPPORT YOU AND THE KIDS WHILE WORKING MINIMUM WAGE AND PAYING CHILD SUPPORT? BITCH I CAN'T EAT! HOW CAN I SUPPORT SOMETHING YOU WON'T LET ME SEE?

At this rate, I will never move out of my mom house. Even worse I will never buy my mom a house. I give up! You win...

CHILD SUPPORT HAS BEEN DIVIDING THE BLACK FAMILY FOR YEARS. WILL IT EVER STOP?

K.O.

Hard times got me moving like a fiend,
I'm going through my closet trying to sell all my things,
I need all the money I can get at the moment,
My mood is "eggs" based on how I am scrambling for dollars,
Maxed out on credit cards,
Defaulting on loans,
No one's fault but my own;

In this fight with life,
I just got knocked the fuck out.

WHEN SHIT HIT THE FAN, GET BACK UP AND GET BACK IN THE FIGHT!

MY MENTAL BREAKDOWN

I reached my breaking point, I can't take it anymore,
I'm packing up all my shit,
Filling up empty bins with all my clothes,
Where am I headed?

Lord knows
With a half tank of gas,
$88 in the stash,
Wherever I go, it won't be far,
I probably just drive until the gas runs out,
And just sleep in my car...

Until further notice,
My marathon continues...

WHEN YOU REACH THIS POINT IN LIFE IT TEACHES YOU HOW TO
APPRECIATE THE SMALLEST THINGS. LIFE WILL ALWAYS FIND A
WAY TO HUMBLE YOU.

INVISIBLE MAN

I'm just existing,
I'm not living,
I'm mentally tripping,
It's like nobody see me,
It's like nobody feel me,
It's like nobody hear me,
As if I'm invisible,
I am addicted to attention,
I must do something to be seen,
I'll do anything for a "Red Heart",
I'll do anything for a "Blue thumb",
I'll do anything for an "Eyeball",
That is why you see me acting crazy on social media,
I'm trying to go viral,
I crave the stage.

NOTE TO READER: MAKE SURE YOU ARE THE SAME PERSON OFF
THE STAGE AS YOU ARE ON THE STAGE.

STILL NIGGA (JUST LIKE YOU)

It happens to me too,
I am also a victim of this system,
My skin color makes me guilty by association,
I don't get a pass,
Just because I wear a badge,
Out of uniform, I get randomly pulled over for no reason
JUST LIKE YOU,
I get asked to step out the vehicle JUST LIKE YOU,
I get profiled for no reason JUST LIKE YOU,
I get followed around the store JUST LIKE YOU,
My house cost more for no reason JUST LIKE YOU,
My job application goes to the bottom of the stack JUST LIKE YOU,
I get killed for no reason JUST LIKE YOU,
I had to go through the fire JUST LIKE YOU,
Even though I swore to protect and serve,
America still treats me like a nigga
JUST LIKE YOU.

We are one and the same.

*Black men in authority are not safe from the stereotypes of America.

FAMILY

We can't choose what family we are born into. We only get one. They love you unconditionally no matter what, and they will be there when you fall. Through the ups and down, just love them. There is nothing like family. I love being a Brown. I wouldn't change it for the world.

LINDA'S KIDS

I'm the third oldest of four,
Basically, the second youngest,
Mama has this saying...
Don't fuck with her money,
Don't fuck with her kids,
Don't fuck with her;

She will do anything for us,
Ms. Linda loves her kids.

MY SIBLINGS

MENTAL NOTES, DULY NOTED

I heard what you said about me,
You tried to diminish my character,
For your personal gain,
My truth needs no lawyer,
It stands firm on its square,
So, when I heard the shit you kicked, I didn't even get mad,
I just learned the true nature of the devil in you,
I filed the information in my mental Rolodex,
I tried to keep it black and white between us,
But, I see your true colors now,
That makes it difficult for me to deal with you.

P.S: I was too good to the people that you tried to get to turn on me.
That is why they didn't. Loyalty runs deep, and I have a good name in
this game.

MIND READER

Surrounded by Human Puzzles,
Mentally, I solve them on a daily basis,
I feel as though I am a reincarnation of a prior being,
I feel as though I already know individuals I encounter,
I have a keen eye for ulterior motives,
I see the devil in the slightest actions,
Save that game for what's his name.

MAMA KNOWS BEST

My girl and my mom told me to watch my friends,
Never play them close,
Only trust them far as I can throw them,
With that logic, I can only trust you while in your presence.
Me being myself though, I gave y'all the benefit of the doubt,
They don't know y'all like I do,
But moms seen this episode before,
She said in time you will see, son;

Now, Product is Missing,
Money isn't adding up,
Rumors are spreading,
Hate is brewing,
Mama was right all along,
Them niggas was riding my wave just to get to shore,
Lesson Learned: Feed people with a long spoon,
I'm sorry, Mama.

A MOTHER CAN SEE THE END BEFORE THE BEGINNING. USE HER
WORDS AND WISDOM TO MANUEVER THROUGH LIFE. A MOTHER
KNOWS.

IF YOU MUST KNOW

You found out how much I make by mistake,
Now, you are clocking my dough,
You ask to borrow money and got mad when I said "No",
I don't have it, but I mean – I do,
It's just not for you,
My bills are my priority at the moment,
I have no free money just to give,
Now, you want to threaten to kick me out,
All because I can't get afford to help you out,
I'm grown and don't have to explain shit…

But, if you must know:

- I owe USAA bank $3,100 because I over drafted in Vegas. I lost 5k shooting craps.
- I am paying $2,500 monthly for my bills at home (Rent, Car Note, Car Insurance, Electric, Gas).
- My Navigator went to collections. I owe $2,700. They call me daily.
- I owe five people $1,600 in total. I have shit to pay. That's why I don't have $20 to give you to get your fucking nails done.

MESSAGE: KEEP YOUR SALARY AND WAGES TO YOURSELF. YOU TELL SOMEONE YOUR HOURLY WAGE AND THEY WILL CALCULATE IT TO THE TEE. FOR EXAMPLE, IF YOU MAKE $10 AN HOUR, THAT IS $1,600 A MONTH BEFORE TAXES. LET'S SAY YOUR TOTAL MONTHLY BILLS TOTAL UP TO $950. IN THE EYES OF THE PERSON ASKING YOU FOR MONEY YOU HAVE AN EXTRA $650 LEFT, AND THAT WILL BE THEIR JUSTIFICATION TO WHY YOU SHOULD JUST GIVE THEM YOUR MONEY BECAUSE YOU SIMPLY HAVE IT. YOU WILL LOSE MANY FRIENDS AND FAMILY THIS WAY. NO ONE IS EXEMPT. PACE YOURSELF!

BROTHERLY LOVE

This poem is called Brotherly Love,
I wrote it for the brother I love,
You set the bar getting married,
Like Tupac said, "I ain't mad at cha"
As long as you are happy, that's all that matters,
Fuck the world.

MY BROTHER AND I AT HIS WEDDING

FATHER

Subconsciously, every man lives to satisfy the expectations of his father. His opinions and thoughts weigh the most during the adolescence phase during childhood. Most of us never had one though.

FATHERLESS

I never met you. Where are you? What's your excuse? I mastered the art of lying, so please justifying 26 years of total absence. Are you a magician? If not, then maybe the hide and seek world champion. I have been looking for you all my life. I'm still looking. I don't even know where to start honestly.

Were you scared of a child? I was too, shit; I even killed a few of my own. I wasn't ready, and I knew that. I understand why you skipped town when you had me. I'm trying to track you down and learn some life lessons from you. Where are you?

Were my cries like mosquitoes buzzing in your ear? Is that why you swatted me out of your life? I know you feel empty knowing you have a son out here raising himself. Mom has been holding it down though. She kept me on the straight and narrow. She tried to at least. My whole crew was fatherless. That made us closer as young men being raised in the jungle.

IN THE HOOD, A GROUP OF FRIENDS USUALLY HAVE ONE THING IN COMMON THAT KEEPS THEM TOGETHER. WE ALL HAD STRONG SINGLE MOTHERS AND NO FATHERS. THAT MADE US BROTHERS IN A SENSE.

26 YEARS

One thing about time is that is sure does fly by,
Babies are born,
Men die,
We Cry, and Move On,
As Life does,
No Time for Regrets or "What Ifs",
Go for what you know,
Use your losses as lessons,
I'm 26 now, and we finally spoke,
You justified your excuse in your absence,
It is what it is,
I'm not picking sides, I'm just happy the wound is healed,
I can't blame you for my future mishaps and misfortunes,
Since I know you now,
I feel like I was in a video game before I met you, but since we
reunited, You have been sort of a health pack,
I was slowly dying out here,
We have a lot to catch up on,
I don't take anything face value,
So, before I humble my stubbornness and call you "Dad",
We need to take a blood test,
Results are in,
You have .001 chance of being my Biological Father!
The search continues...

FRIENDS

At first you and your friends start off as a unit. You do everything together – Party, Club, Drink, Study, and plan futures as a team. As time takes its toll, you will branch off into your true calling.

RULES TO RULE

Friends come and go,
Trust no one,
Take nothing face value,
Question everything,
Do the knowledge,
Create lasting memories,
Take your secrets to the grave.

LETTER TO MY FRIENDS

Stop calling me to Party!
Call me to make some Money!
What are we celebrating? Why are we here?
For the price of 1, I just paid for six beers,
We are victims, we are consumers,
We need to change our thinking, and become the producers,
So, we can profit off people's miscellaneous nonsense,
We are on the wrong end of the stick,
It's always pimping in progress...

PS: WHEN I SAY IT IS ALWAYS "PIMPING" IN PROGRESS, IT SIMPLY
MEANS I AM CONSTANTLY LOOKING FOR WAYS TO MAKE MONEY
WITHOUT DOING PHYSICAL LABOR OR THE WORK PERIOD. I RATHER
WORK FROM THE NECK UP. LIFE IS A THINKING MAN'S GAME. THE
BRAIN IS THE STRONGEST MUSCLE. USE IT. EXERCISE IT.

Keep Running...

THE SALMON ASSASSIN

I'm rocking the pink suit with the yellow guts,
It's my birthday and I don't give a fuck,
I'm the cleanest motherfucker in this party,
I see the ladies peeking,
But, they aren't speaking,
They are in a daze,
Fresh shave got me looking 21 again,
Cougars are choosing,
I'm Just enjoying myself,
Tonight, I am not hunting,
I'll leave that to the Huntsmen,
They are always out for blood,
I'm going to just chill in the cut,
Just two step and sip my drink,
Nod my head to the smooth tunes,
I'm quiet money in the purest form,
Happy 25th to me.

THE HUNTSMEN AND I CELEBRATING MY 25TH BIRTHDAY IN
CHARLOTTE, NC.

I'M GOOD

Just got this new job,
I'm thankful for the blessing,
My boys hit me up, asked if I wanted to chip in on a section,
$2,100 for a few hours,
All we get is a couch and a few bottles,
Split it 4 ways and that's $525 a man,
Wisdom settling in as I rationalize with the man within,
My thoughts are as follows:
My rent is $1,104 and paying that allows me to live for 31 days,
$1,104 divided by 31 is $35 per day,
So, $525 divided by $35 is 15 days of living,
In exchange for a night out,
It's not adding up,
I'm good phellas,
I hope y'all enjoy yourselves,
Be safe.

Pay Bills	Party
· Roof Over Head for 31 days · Have extra money for miscellaneous charges · Have extra money for rainy days	· Get Drunk · Risk Getting a DUI on way home · Further kill my Liver · Risk waking up to a girl I wouldn't normally talk to

WHEN YOU GO BROKE YOU START CALCULATING EVERYTHING TO THE TEE. I DON'T BLAME YOU! MAKE IT MAKE SENSE.

MONEY

Is money the root of all-evil? Or, is it the need and greed of it? Money can make you or break you. Have you up or down depending on the amount you have. I understand all thought processes when it comes to money. Here are my stories.

THE LEMONADE THEORY

"The sole purpose of life is to make lemonade. We are born with the lemons, which are ambition and drive. Instead of using our innate lemons to make lemonade, we often settle for a damn soda!"

If you have a certain talent, athletic ability, specific skillset, make sure you get paid what you weigh. Don't get tricked out of well-deserved pay due to lack of work or opportunities available. Create your own jobs and fulfill your own destiny.

Example: I know this guy who can cook! When I say he can cook, he can make anything from scratch and the presentation of the food is up to par with most five-star restaurants. He served a few years in prison and was labeled a felon in the eyes of America. After countless jobs turned him down due to his criminal background, he fell into a slight depression. He eventually found employment at a gym and ended up miserable living paycheck to paycheck. The jewel I am attempting to bestow on you is: Use your talents to make a better life for you the best way possible. If the front door of the house of opportunity is locked, try the back door, and if that door is locked, go on the side of the house and check the windows. If those windows are locked, then get a ladder and try the upstairs windows including the bathroom. However, when you get in, leave it open for the next man to be granted access to manifest his personal goals. It's enough money for everyone to benefit. Never give up!

Note to Reader: If you don't use your lemons (Talents) to make your own lemonade (Business), someone else will use your lemonade (Skills) and chase their vodka with it. It happens on a daily basis. Basically, the owner of a business will hire the brightest and smartest individuals to work at his company all while he sits on the beach with his swimming trunks and his debit card.

CAN YOU RELATE?

Bills on Bills on Bills, a blank page is my will, I can barely afford to live.

So, when I pass on to the next life, did I die for free? I couldn't escape the cycle. I'm sorry, son. I apologize, and you are not even here yet.

Every day, I am trying to make a way for you although you are just a thought in my head. It is hard out here. I hesitate to manifest you in the physical form because there is a war going and we are getting slaughtered daily.

The women are temporary, so they come and go. It is hard to decipher who is there for me and who isn't. The more I let them get to know me, the more they walk away. My psyche is outside the norm of mere mortals. I see too deep, and I see too much. I yearn for the deep conversation but always end up keeping it surface level.

I am addicted to my freedom, but often it gets lonely in the wind. Do I need enough money to accommodate a travel partner or just hunt when I get to my destination?

Wise man says "Be the change you want to see" so I must set the example of what I want to see in everyday society. I will be the first of my crew to get married and restore the structure of the diminished black family.

I need to allow someone to get to know me while I am in the process of becoming me, because after the money starts rolling in and the accolades start to pile up it will be hard to find a good woman while avoiding gold diggers.

Do you feel me?

THOUGHTS OF A GEE

Time is Money, and Money is Time. Well, I need money, so I can buy time to escape life for a few months. Shit, maybe longer.

If I could get paid to travel, you would never see me again. I belong to the desert, and I live in the wind. The World is mine.

Nobody wants to work; we all hate the new plantation setup. Back then, we could leave the plantation when we stomached up the courage to escape towards freedom and happiness. My have the tables turned.

Today we are free to do whatever we choose to, but subconsciously we are slaves to our jobs and build our lives around it. We don't move unless it is for the money. Money is our only motivation. Love doesn't live here anymore.

We are slowly getting back to uniting as a people. We are waking up and realizing the true enemy. The further I look back into history, the more I understand why things are the way they are.

I advise you to read books!

EVENTUALLY

Stressed out to the max,
Bills are on my back,
Once I clear a debt,
A new one arises,
All I can do is work and stay on the clock,
Eventually, I'll pay this shit off.

UNTITLED

What a day,
What a week,
What a month,
What a year it's been,
I've cut off some of my closest friends,
Few cousins passed away due to senseless violence,
I'm still unemployed,
I'm still playing with my girl's emotions,
All my hustles dried up,
Only thing I have going for me is this book,
I hope it all works out.

CATFISHED

I need a drink,
I can't even think,
I close my eyes and extend the blink,
Meditate on better days for a minute,
Then open my eyes to deal with reality,
AZ said, "A person's status depends on salary",
With that being said,
I am on the same level as a catfish,
Bottom of the barrel,
I have to get my money up.

HUSTLING

There is big difference between a drug dealer and a hustler. There is a specific science and art when it comes to the hustle. Most people consume while the hustler produces. Most people demand while the hustler supplies. Would you rather be the on the receiving end of funds or the one always on the buying end? Pick a side.

THE HUSTLER'S CREED

I pledge allegiance to the creed of the Hustler,
I pledge to see the world for what it is,
And, to view all humans as customers,
I am not a consumer, I am a producer,
If I consume, it is only to produce on the back end,
I have no ulterior motive,
My intention is only to profit,
If one hustle dries out,
I pledge to reinvent myself to further ensure income,
I don't believe in droughts,
Every Human has demands,
I pledge to supply them,
The nature of the hustler is a science,
I pledge to analyze all information obtained and apply it to the best of
my knowledge,
If I don't hustle I don't eat,
Only the strong survive, no pity for the weak,
I pledge to hustle hard no matter what,
A dollar earned is a dollar I didn't have,
I pledge to never let money walk away,
If I must sell a product for the same price I paid for it; then, so be it,
I made my money back at least,
This is how I rationalize with self,
The universal motto of the hustler is to:
"Learn and Earn",
Let's Get It.

WHAT THE FUCK AM I THINKING?

Did I jump into a relationship too quick?
I still have a list of chicks I want to hit,
In reality, them bitches ain't shit,
What the fuck am I thinking?
I have a new job making $2,000 a week,
But, still want to make money in the streets,
Meeting millionaires left and right and they are telling me the legal life is where it's at,
But, the streets are like a monkey on my back,
I can't get out,
I'm mentally trapped,
Every dollar I'm thinking about a quick flip,
Instead of wise investments so I can be legit,
What the fuck am I thinking?
The road less traveled is empty,
Easy way is full of accidents,
Because everyone is stuck in traffic,
Trying to co-exist in a world that yearns individualism,
Trying to fit in is Suicide,
Go with your Gut and Do You!

Keep Running...

THE WORLD THROUGH MY EYES

Analyzing the world, I see that we lost our way. No anchor, no culture, no morals, no foundation, no respect, and no love. People are just riding trends. They are balloons out here. They go wherever the wind blows. This is why there is so much traffic now because everyone is swerving and merging into lanes they don't belong in. Stay solid and keep it one thousand because a hundred isn't enough anymore!

HUSTLING BACKWARDS

I'm in the club with bottles popping,
I haven't paid my car note in 4 months,
My credit dropping,
My Life flopping,
It is true when they say,
You win some and lose some,
I am a true hustler,
I know many ways to generate some income,
I constantly talk myself out of ideas I come up with,
I probably could have been a billionaire by now,
I need help,
My pride won't let me ask for it,
I blame my past for it,
I've always had money; at least that what people thought,
So, when I ask, they think I am joking,
So, I carry on,
All alone,
My marathon continues...

P.S.: When people say that you can call them when you need "anything" they don't mean anything. You can only call for advice, and 9 times out of 10 you probably told yourself all the advice that the person is telling you. When you call them for money, things go awry like plans of mice and men. Save your money is the advice I have for you.

ASS BACKWARDS

You are on the football field setting picks,
You are on the basketball court with cleats on,
You are golfing with a soccer ball,
You are playing tennis with volleyballs,
You don't know what game you are playing,
That is why you are losing,
Pick a lane and put 10,000 hours in,
Study, Learn, and Apply,
Mastery is the mission of life.

STINKING THINKING

I've been paying car insurance for years,
Never got in an accident,
Basically, money down the drain,
No return on my investment,
Not a penny,
Insurance is the scam of all scams,
I am about to crash my car on purpose,
Maybe have it stolen strategically,
Make them cut me a blank check,
Fuck the increase of my monthly payments,
What's an extra $40 – $50?
When I can get a $10,000 lump sum after appraisal,
After the insurance check clears,
Cancel the policy,
Get back on mom's,
Is this stinking thinking?
Or a valid hustle?

NOTE TO READER: You pay $200 a month for insurance. Multiply that by 12 and that comes out to $2400 annually. Keep that same payment for 20 years and you will end up paying $48,000. If no accidents occur in that time span, in my eyes you wasted income. Crash that car and get you a check for a few grand!

P.S Please don't crash your car literally. I don't want to be the reason behind it, but just trying to show you how this is a scam.

PLAY TO WIN...

If you lose,
Play Again,
Never Stop Halfway,
Play Until the End,
See it through,
It's Worth It.

WHY I TRAP

I trap because I am good at it,
I trap because it is easy,
I trap because it is convenient,
It's all I know honestly,
I am a product of my environment,
My life is wrinkled,
I don't plan on ironing shit,
Family constantly telling me to get a job,
What I'll make in a week,
I can make in an hour,
It doesn't make sense to work;

So, if you want me to retire from these streets,
You must present a legal opportunity with the same profits,
Until then,
I'm trapping.

THE SKY (INSPIRED BY FLOYD MAYWEATHER)

I pat both pockets and conclude that I'm broke as shit. All around me I see bad chicks and niggas with nice whips. I'm living paycheck-to-paycheck...

What the fuck am I doing wrong? I mean seriously; I completed your High School requirements and graduated from your esteemed University (CAU), but one question remains. Where the hell is the money? They say the higher the degree the higher the salary, right?

It took me almost a year to find work and now I'm ducking Sallie Mae because I ain't got it dog. Opportunity knocks often but the job description throws me off.

I tell myself "man I can't do that or I lack the experience and give up on some little boy shit, then escape reality by picking up a joystick and play 2k. I admit I am wasting time.

Life is short and each funeral brings me closer to death. I cry, look at the sky; ask am I next? When I come to, I question life and ask why take my closest friends and keep me here?

All I do is mistreat women, read books, work, party, and drink beer.

I will soon find a purpose and live for it.

As for you, I see you stunting in traffic, switching lanes with that bad chick. I admit I am jealous, but I am not hating.

I justify your success with the following statement: He just has more access to information. He knows something I don't.

You see, I do not hate and only I know why. Honestly, I admire seeing you fly, because when I figure this shit out and earn my wings, I will fly right next to you.

It's room for all of us in the sky.

Keep Running...

You motivate me. You give me reassurance that it is more to life than mingling with the mortals, and there is life off of the ground. I'll keep running and eventually Level Up.

Never base your success off the success of others! Remember: The tortoise won the race, not the hare!

Please, Pace Yourself.

THE STREETS

The streets do not love anyone, but we love the streets. During the duration of my marathon, I have seen many sides of the game. I have seen some of the best hustlers fall victim to the prison system and some of the toughest guys die. I have been to six times more funerals than weddings thus far. These are my thoughts.

WAS IT WORTH IT?

You killed him to be labeled "real" in the eyes of me,
You broke into houses in the name of "putting food on the table for your family",
You are out here just to be out here,
Can you explain why?
You stole money from your mother's purse knowing it was for the rent,
You jumped into that car with your boys knowing a drive by would soon occur,
You bullied weaker kids to feed your ego,
You stole clothes just to sell them to your friend's half price,
You had a good crime spree up until you got caught,
Now look at you with your head down in front of the judge,
Hoping for remorse, and expecting him to show you some love,
When he banged the gavel and sentenced you to 10 years mandatory,
You heard someone in the courtroom ask: Was it worth your life?
The answer is "NO!"
In the pot of life everything boils down to
CHOICES, CHOICES, CHOICES!!!...

Keep Running...

JUST ANOTHER DAY

Gunshots rang out and we knew more were soon to follow,
Still we sat on the block chilling,
Sharing a pint of Hennessey,
Venting to each other about our problems with the world,
Until intoxicated then we try to find some girls,
Sex heals depressed men like us temporarily,
Until I wake up due to the haunting of my dreams and goals,
They are like chains on my brain,
And they won't go away until they are manifested,
I can bullshit the homies all day,
But I can no longer lie to myself,
I'm tired of sitting on the block,
It's go time,
I'm going home to type my book.

BALLOON STRINGS

You don't care about my girlfriend,
You answer when I call every time,
The phone barely rings,
You fuck and suck me on command at my convenience,
I love when you visit I can't lie,
You don't even trip or complain about why we can't be together,
You understand,
You play your position well,
You know not to call me,
We only talk when I reach out,
Might be days or weeks between each conversation,
You don't mind,
In the moments of my absence it makes you miss me more,
That makes everything better,
Unfortunately, this must stop,
I'm sorry this is so sudden,
I'm in good hands now,
I value our friendship outside of sex,
We will remain friends until the end if that's cool,
You can call for advice and wisdom any time,
I have one last request though,
Let's fuck one more time,
Let's record it on your phone,
So, you can watch when you think of me,
Can you dig that?
If not,
Give me my shovel back!
We both been holding it down like balloons,
But all balloons must be set free.

EVERY MAN HAS TO CUT TIES WITH ALL HIS OTHER WOMEN WHEN
HE MEETS THE RIGHT ONE. NO IFS, ANDS, OR BUTS! NO EXCEPTIONS.

THE TRANSPORTER

Traveling the world in search of a connect,
It's a drought in the hood I am from,
Prices are sky high, everybody taxing,
The violence rate is rising as well,
Made a few phone calls and inquires,
Accumulated some valid information,
It's ShowTime; Time for me to get in the wind,
Rolling solo, I don't need a co-defendant,
I'm not telling on myself,
Upon my arrival, the product looks good as advertised,
I crunch numbers in my head to estimate my profits,
Time to flood the town now,
Quick prayer before I jump on the highway,
Lord knows I'm just hustling to fund my second life,
I have to get this book out,
No handouts for a black man,
I have a plan, just no upfront money,
No cash in the stash and my credit won't get it,
So, having good intentions and making bad decisions,
Is me rationalizing with self about my actions,
Long ride ahead of me,

I made it back safe and sound,
It's go time,
All hail the transporter.

YOU CAN MAKE SHITLOADS OF MONEY MULING PRODUCT. IF YOU
GET CAUGHT, JUST BE PREPARED FOR THE CONSEQUENCES.

FROM A WORKING MAN

I make $1,600 a week,
You make $1,600 a day,
Honestly, I wouldn't have it any other way,
Nothing like consistent slow money,
It's a lot that comes with getting that Good ol' dope money,
I rather deal with petty coworkers from 9 to 5,
Than deal with stink fiends who rob, steal and lie,
If my check is short for whatever reasons,
HR will be quick to fix it,
But, when your runners come up short on a pack,
You take the loss and charge it to business,
After I get off work I go home and rest,
You have to be out all night and wear a bulletproof vest,
When I die my benefits will take care of my family,
When you die we have to throw a fish fry and start a go fund me to
bury you,
Wise Up, Life is Short,
Play to Win,
Leave them streets alone,
I love you,
I would hate to lose you to these streets,
I lost so many friends and family members thus far,
Respect me for trying to reinvent the wheel,
I'm praying for you.

PATIENCE

Jamaican music exits the speaker and fills the space we are
occupying,
Your body is moving to the beat in symphony,
I'm observing from the cut just 2 stepping and nodding my head,
Watching you block shots the various men are shooting,
9 up and 9 down,
I laugh to myself while I sip my Hennessy,
"Tough cookie" I say to myself,
My legs decided to walk over to you,
So, my upper body was forced to follow,
We notice each other,
We are locking eyes and time stops,
I can't hear any music now,
I snap out of the daze and say to her,
"Studies show that 1 out of 10 men will dance with you tonight,"
I saw you curve 9 lames tonight, so it must be my lucky day, huh?
I'm the last one, baby; Lucky number 10,
Intrigued by my wittiness and quick thinking,
She smiles and begins to whine on me so slow and seductively,
Soon a crowd forms and cheers us on,
Through my shades I see them 9 lames hating,
I'm strapped,
I am not tripping,
I have some advice for them:

Respect the Player and the Game,
It will reward you,
Results vary.

In small towns, most patrons in the clubs mean mug and start drama
for no reason. I can't explain why, I just know how to carry myself in a
matter that avoids confrontation.

Keep Running...

I SAVED YOUR LIFE

You was low on cash,
You were fucked up in the game,
I built you a bridge to get back on your feet,
You had an ulterior motive though,
You used my name for personal gain,
My face card was the only reason you were given the product on consignment,
You didn't have to lift a finger,
I handled all logistics of the operation,
All it took was one day,
After the drop off you said you needed a few days to move the work,
Then you would send the money back,
Few days go by,
You made a payment and was $500 short,
Then changed your number and deleted all your social media,
I asked around, nobody has seen you,
The bridge is trembling due to your actions,
You fucked me over, and took advantage of me,
You don't care, Life Goes On
I loved you though; let me tell you how much,
My man was pissed about the $500 he never received,
The transaction took place at your mother's house,
He kept the text messages, so he still had the address,
He was ready to kill everyone in the house, including you if you were there,
Better be happy he consulted with me first,
I said, "Don't Do It",
Let him Live,
He has many kids,
I don't want them to grow up fatherless like I did,
I'll take a $500 pay cut on the next operation I put together,
One hand washes the other,
It's been a year and still no payment,
You are physically alive, but dead to me,
So next time you brag about fucking me over to them hoes,
Keep Running...

Just know,
The only reason you are living is because I didn't push the button,
I SAVED YOUR LIFE!

LIFE IN THE HOOD (PICTURE THIS)

I'm chilling on the stoop,
Old heads driving Cadillac's and rocking linen suits,
Pimps are in high pursuit for brand new prostitutes,
The young-ins on payroll ready to shoot,
Grams calling to talk to me about god,
But, I lost faith a long time ago,
I can hear the preacher up the street preaching,
Nobody is listening,
The babies are playing barefoot and only wearing diapers,
The candy lady is knocking on doors collecting credit,
The police are fucking with everyone,
They are bored,
Moms is cooking,
I can smell the food through the door,
That's a typical day in the hood,
Outsiders say we are dumb,
They say we won't finish high school,
We have no knowledge,
Slim to none are our chances of ever going to college,
Single mothers raise us; we have no fathers,
This is everyday life here;

In your eyes, Life is far from the norm,
We are roses that grew from concrete,
Either we weather the storm, or drown trying,
We must rise above this area,
There is more to life,
We know it, just no positive examples around to follow.

PRINCIPLES

I am contemplating killing my childhood friend over $500,
Logics steps in and tells me "let it slide,
I can't; I'm filled with pride,
How he going to play me like that?
He fucked up the pack,
He said he would pay me right back,
Time goes by,
Almost two years,
At this point I'm ready to kill,
Let everyone know I'm real,
The only thing stopping me is having your mother deal with the pain,
And, your son growing up without a father like I did,
I'm charging you and the $500 to the game,
When you see me, just know you lost a good friend,
When business begins, friendship ends,
I learned that from Pimpin' Ken.

"If you aren't going to kill him over the money let him keep it if he
owe." – Jadakiss

HARD TIME

You did the crime,
Now you have to serve that time,
10 years,
Look behind you,
Wave goodbye to your wife,
You see them tears fall from her eye,
As they haul you off to your new room,
Inside the concrete mansion,
Thoughts racing through your mind,
It seems unreal,
Living 100mph and finally slowed down,
The irony is that the faster you live,
The faster you make it to the stop sign,
Hold your head up in there,
See you when you get out,
In the streets there is a saying, "If it isn't life it isn't long",
Do the time do not let the time do you.

FACE CARD

This poem is about "Respect",
Someone sends money to a person they never met,
I vouched for both parties,
I built the bridge,
One had the product,
One had the customers,
The rest is history,
I don't want to be compensated for my connection,
Just keep my name good,
I might need you as a reference,
For the next operation I come up with,
Stay safe.

ALL ACROSS THE WORLD, THERE ARE MIDDLEMEN PROFITING OFF
THIS SIMPLE FORMULA.

BY ANY MEANS

You don't understand,
You lack experience,
You can't relate to this shit I'm dealing with,
I went from being on top of my world,
To being financially dependent on my girl,
I have no car, no consistent income,
I guess I win some and I lose some,
You are not from where I'm from,
You haven't seen what I seen,
You don't understand the logic of "by any means",
I'm not scared of jail; I've been twice,
It's my world; everyone just exists in it.

PULLING THE PLUG

What is in question is my sanity,
I've lost 95% of my faith in humanity,
No love here,
Niggas ain't shit,
Been a player to long,
I can't trust any chick,
Everybody Hustling,
Everybody Struggling,
Family not the same anymore,
They use you like the next man,
They don't appreciate the dots I connected,
It is disrespectful how my effort is not respected,
I am pulling the plug on all bridges I built,
I'm making you get it from another person,
All this money being made on my face card and I can't eat?
N***a Please,
Watch this.

Note to Reader: When you are running your circus (operation) of whatever it may be that you are doing, just know this. Never give up your formula to success to anyone. Employ people and put them where you need them. One monkey will stop the show depending the position held. Hire wisely. Play to win.

THE SPOOK WHO SAT BY THE DOOR

I'm playing dumb on the job,
Even though I am the smartest person in the building,
I'm stealing the game from Peter,
And bringing it back to Paul,
Never outshine the master,
That's the 1st law of power,
Fuel his ego while setting up your move,
He won't see it coming,
It will be too late when he realizes it,
I'm no Uncle Tom,
I'm just playing my role,
I'm in character from 9 to 5,
Once I get in the house of opportunity,
I will leave the back door open for you,
We infiltrate from the ground up,
Then we take this building my storm,
Are you with me?

When you see a black man high in a position, don't automatically write him off as an Uncle Tom. He might be just playing possum until the opportunity to execute his plan presents itself. Just remain calm and stay patient. Time will answer your questions.

FAKE LOVE

Surrounded by fake love and opportunists who just want to ride my wave,
I keep them in the water treading,
Why would I bring them to shore?
They don't love me,
They just love what I do for them,
Maybe if I fake falling off,
They will jump off my boat and reveal their true colors and intentions,
Actions speak louder than words,
Time will answer all questions.

WHAT AM I THINKING?

Feeding my ego and not giving a damn about people,
It's my way or the highway,
I am the loner, the traveling man,
Currently, sitting stationary waiting on a plantation to call,
When they do, I'll become an actor and play the slave with a ulterior motive,
I know why I am here; To fund my second life,
How about you? You like your job or are you just dependent on the paycheck?
Honestly, I'm addicted to the hustle,
Buying low and selling high,
Researching consumers demands so I can supply,
My priorities are scrambled,
I don't know what's important anymore,
Mom wants me to get a Job ASAP,
Friends want to party and drink daily,
Paranoia got me seeking solitude in,
Crowded places,
In glass Hennessy Bottles,
Crap tables,
I'm looking everywhere but in the mirror,
I have to rid my conscience of suppressed desires and find ways to release my demons,
If I don't I will lose the closest things to me and I don't want that to occur.

Where do you go to find yourself?

Keep Running...

SEX

Sex is a beautiful thing.

Be safe, THOUGH.

Enjoy....

SALT AND PEPPER

By the way that you are sucking me, I can tell that you are in love with me. Slow down though, I am warning you. I am about to explode, and if you don't slow down it's going to be all over your nose. Don't get mad either; because you've been told.

Mhm Mhm Mhm. Damn! It's too late. Shit, My bad. I know you felt my leg shaking. That was your warning….

Don't storm off to the bathroom like you mad as shit. In ten minutes, I will be hard again and will need you to ride this dick. Damn, you still mad? Well, let me taste it and you can bust on my face in the name of revenge. Lay back and look at the ceiling and enjoy the feeling of this sexual healing.

I noticed the anticipation in her eyes. I quickly and precisely aim and jam Roscoe in her! It went in first try. If I would've missed, she would've got up and stopped me. She moans out, "But bae, I thought you were gone eat me out?

Haaa, Got Eeeem!!!

I say "Sike Naw"; you really want me to stop stroking you? Shiiidd…I'm already in this thang. Turn around real quick. You know I won't be back here too long. You got that "2 stroke murder she wrote" pussy. It kills me every time. RIP Me.

Until Next time…

SALT AND PEPPER (REMIX)

You ass-naked walking around my house,
That's what the fuck I am talking about,
You know what you doing and so do I,
I'm playing your game girl with the universal joystick of life,

See, you think I don't know you naked under my hoodie,
I see your fingers all wet from playing in them goodies,
Girl stop playing, bring me that pussy,
I'm playing with my beard and licking my lips, staring at you in the
mirror all thick and shit,

My dick saying "Fuck Food",
My stomach screaming, "I'm hungry though",
In my mind, I know "out" is where she wants to go,
Plus, I hit it twice earlier - I couldn't get hard if I wanted to,
Fuck it - Let me get my ass dressed!

Keep Running...

IT HAPPENS TO THE BEST OF US

Looking down at you while you sucking my dick,
I'm slowly dying, you sucking the life out my shit,
Slurping and Burping,
Burping and Slurping,
And at the same time,
Simultaneously Jerking,
My Toes Curling,
My Body Shivering,
My Soul Tingling,
Talking to myself like "WTF",
You can't nut yet,
You didn't even fuck yet,
Talking all that shit on the phone,
Now look at you,
I tell her slow down, but she speeds up,
I'm thinking about basketball,
While at the same time squeezing my butt,
All in attempt to hold back this nut,
It didn't work; I ended up busting in her mouth,
Most of it was on her; the rest was on the couch,
I died for 5 seconds,
When I came back to life,
She was on all 4's and said, "You better do me right",
I'm sitting there in shrimp mode,
Hold up, I need ten minutes baby!

RED HUARACHES

I open the door and I'm surprised,
You ass naked with red huaraches on,
That's the shit that turns me on,
You know that's my favorite color right?
I look down at Roscoe,
He on 10, Harder than a roll of quarters,
Grab my hand baby, lead me upstairs,
Watch out for the dog though,
Lock her out,
I don't need a witness for all this freakiness that's about to occur,
Lay down on the bed love,
Daddy hungry,
Let me taste that fat cat,
Let me treat that clit like a lollipop from the bank,
Look down at me as I look up to you,
Let's wink at each other in unison,
As I snicker to myself as I return back to my meal,
I lick my lips as I come up,
I'm so horny, I want to skip getting head,
Charge it to the game,
It's a sex write off,
I check my watch – it's missionary time,
Slow passionate strokes as we stare into each other's eyes,
I love participating in this sacred transaction of bodily fluids with you,
Turn around,
It's ShowTime,
Throw that ass back like we playing catch,
Let me freestyle over the acapella of that ass clapping against my nuts,
UH OH!
I feel a tingle building up,
Here it cums,
Shows Over,
You thirsty?

Keep Running...

WHAT'S UP, BABY?

I see you peeking, but you not speaking,
Don't be shy; I don't bite.
Talk to me, I'll talk back,
What is your name?
What do they call you?
What do you do when the sun is shining?
She giggles to herself,
She is feeling me,
I got her,
Soon she will fall right into my Venus flytrap,
Soon she will drop her guard and her heart will be mine,
I just want to experience you a few times and then put you back on the shelf,
Is that cool?

SOMETIMES US MEN SEE A WOMAN AND JUST WANT TO HIT IT AND
GET BACK TO OUR LIVES. EASIER SAID THAN DONE.

WHY WE FUCKING?

Some women will fuck you because of who you are,
Some women will fuck you just because of your job description,
Some women will fuck you just to say they experienced you,
Some women will fuck you and don't even know why,
Some women will fuck you because everyone else wants to or already is.
See yourself how others see you,
Play the hand you were dealt,
The cards vary with each woman,
Just sit back and enjoy the ride,
Play to win and never forget why you are playing.

IS THIS TRUE LADIES?

SUPER SUCKER DELUXE 3000

Let me fuck your face,
Let me thrust your throat,
Not too hard though,
I don't want you to choke,
Breathe through your nose,
But never stop sucking,
Master this technique and you won't have to worry about anything,
I'm staying with you for life,
I want to be the only recipient of this Super Sucker Deluxe 3000
treatment,
Over and out,
Psssh...

WOMEN

"This is a man's world, but it's nothing without a woman"   –
James Brown

You can't live with them, and you can't live without them. These are my experiences.

A LONER AT HEART

All these women in my inbox want relationships,
I just want to binge fuck at my convenience,
I can only fuck you good, that is all I can do for you,
No lovey dove stuff,
That last heartbreak fucked me up,
It's me, not you,
So, don't waste your time helping me unpack my baggage,
Leave my suitcase alone, let time do its job,
I don't trust a soul, not even myself sometimes,
I know for a fact that I will cheat on you when the opportunity comes,
and because I know myself I must conclude that you will too,
I spare you the relationship because I know the ending before the beginning,
You and I will be better off as friends, no strings attached,
See, I tell you upfront because I'm blunt,
So, if you agree and sign this verbal agreement, I don't want to hear that,
"What are we?" and "I'm catching feelings",
I'll immediately drop you and get back in the wind,
I stay with a pocket full of money,
But my soul broke,
Still wise though, thanks to them old folks,
No motive found for the actions I take,
But, I understand why I am this way,
Betrayal from the past blurred the vision for my future,
No eye drops in sight, squinting as I continue on this Marathon,
I have to Pace Myself.

Keep Running...

NEVER AGAIN

Anticipating moves so I can stay steps ahead of you,
I won't fall victim to anyone again,
I bumped my head enough times,
I see the devil in the slightest gestures,
One glimpse is all it takes,
Intuition tells no lie,
My third eye sees far into the 5th dimension,
I've been here before it seems,
But making the same mistakes,
As if I am a newborn,
Losses are all lessons that will sharpen my sword,
My Eulogy is my report card that the critics will grade me on.

YOU GOT ME FUCKED UP

You hot and cold,
You on and off,
You here and there,
I'm everywhere,
Always away trying to put things together,
I consistently need consistency,
To validate that you down for me and rocking with my campaign,
We don't talk everyday, but you want a spot on the team,
I be calling,
You don't answer,
I'm forced to keep one in the chamber,
I won't be the new fool at your convenience.
Since we only talk when I reach out, I am forced to arrive at the
conclusion that we will never, talk again,
I am Ok with that,
We can't prosper if I'm giving 100% and its 0% on your end,
Unfortunately, you got me fucked up!

Foolish pride does a pop-up show in my mind,
Taking over my thoughts and actions,
It seems as if I don't care,
I'm in character,
Feeding off my power over others,
I am evil to the 10th degree,
That's how my girl describes me,
It's a shame she has to deal with me,
Along with my emotions,
They are first cousins,
Always Together,
One has to die,
For this relationship to stay alive.

SWEET NOTHINGS

Send me a picture of you so I can talk to it,
When you don't answer the phone,
When I wake up at 3 in the morning,
And don't want to wake you up,
I will just look at your picture,
Throughout the day when you are busy at work,
I will look at the picture,
When you are in class studying for exams,
I will talk to your picture and wish you the best of luck,
When you are free,
Call me,
I will answer on the first ring!

THE DISAGREEMENT

We arguing,
I Shut Down,
My Mindset: I don't give a fuck now,
You call my name,
My response is "WHAT NOW?"
You are losing me mentally,
My feelings are dying by the minute like cells,
Since the 1st heartbreak, I sentenced my heart to life in jail,
While incarcerated, my heart has been in the hole for years,
Love never visits, so my heart grew colder,
That was 10 years ago, I got older,
To cope; my only defense is my mean mug and this foolish pride,
I'm starting to think, "Showing too much Love is a gateway behavior to suicide",
I see through the fake love and wickedness,
Trust Me,
Game knows Game!

SORRY, NOT SORRY

I had no intentions on getting to know you,
I just wanted to fuck,
After a few times of me blessing that cat,
My spider senses are tingling,
You are getting attached,
That's scares me,
Mentally, I runaway like a fish when someone taps its tank,
I know you like me,
I mean you have reason not to,
But how you love me after 2 weeks?
You don't even know me,
You created a vivid version of me in your mind,
I'm not him love,
I only call when I'm horny,
You answer and pull up,
Then, we fuck,
I don't mind you staying the night,
But, you have to be gone first thing in the morning,
You don't know my favorite color,
You don't know what makes me tick,
The only thing you know about me is "my dick",
But, he has a mind of his own,
He is a whole different person,
It's two sides to me, though,
Which one did you get to know?
You have this vision for us in your future,
I was recently upgraded to boo in your life,
But, on my end I'm still taking it slow,
You hired me when I didn't even apply,
My resume reads "Consistent Convenient Dick Only",
Honestly, I see you as a piece of meat,
I don't need you to be my peace,
Just settle for being my freak,
I understand it's a lack of real men out here,

Keep Running...

You met me and folded up like origami,
I get it, I really do,
But, I'm not that guy,
I'm not the one for you baby,
I'm being honest,
I'm sorry.

I NEED SOME COMPANY

I just want you to come thru and chill,
Turn your phone off,
Don't complain about your bills,
Leave your problems at the door,
I have plenty of my own,
I'm up to my hairline in student loans,
They call me every minute like dope fiends,
Money is their drug of choice though,
I'm not trying to steal your thunder,
Just letting you know that life could be worse,
But, anyway, I'm glad you came,
Let's use each other as temporary escapes,
From our external stressors,
Use your tongue to sign this verbal contract,
Warning: It might not last long,
Let's just enjoy the moment until it vanishes,
Let's get drunk out of our minds,
Let's get high until we can't open our eyes,
Let's watch a movie from the 90's to relive our childhoods,
Let's cheat on our diets for a day and eat junk food,
Let's take a selfie to stamp this moment in time,
Once we snap out of this fantasy world,
Let's go back to just simply existing,
I wish we could stay here forever,
But we can't.

SOMETIMES WE NEED TO BE AROUND PEOPLE WHO GET OUR MINDS
OFF OUR PROBLEMS. I FEEL YOU.

I NEED TO LEARN

I need to learn to see your complaints as requests for love,
I need to stop interrupting you while you vent and just pull you in for a hug,
I'm here to listen and evaluate,
So, I can solve the problem,
So, you can stop trembling like a rattlesnake,
It's a lot going in my life that I am dealing with on my own,
I don't want to put my weight on you; you have your own problems,
So, I keep my problems bottled inside and locked away,
Every time I try to vent I can't think of anything to say,
I have to admit,
I am a loner,
I live in my own world,
I seek advice and never apply it,
I beat to my own drum,
I am a free spirit,
I don't need an anchor,
I need you to move how I move,
Keep all questions to a minimum,
If not, get off my boat,
I'm sorry, I admit,
I need to learn how to love differently.

PRIDE WARS

Sitting in the same house,
We both quiet like crickets in the daytime,
Our pride is in our way,
No one is budging to speak first,
It's so quiet I can hear my ears ringing,
I'm upstairs writing poetry,
You are downstairs watching TV,
I'm wondering how was your day today?
Did you eat today?
I did laundry earlier,
I forgot to wash your work shirts,
I apologize; I will get them on the next load,
Its 11:11 time to make a wish,
I wish we could be happy again,
I have to be at work at 6 am,
I am about to shower and get in bed,
Do not be alarmed at my attempt to cuddle,
Even though we not speaking and beefing,
I want you to know "Brother Brown love you",
Don't ever doubt that.

THE WORLD

You put money in my pocket,
Let me drive the car at my convenience,
Paid all the bills when I lost my job,
You held it down during my unemployment stint,
You loved me through my rough patch,
You supported me though my struggle,
That's why I love you,
In this day and age, nobody doing that from the start,
You are my angel in disguise,
The woman I meditated about,
I would like to thank the universe for answering my prayers,
I want to give you everything you deserve,
Even though the world is already yours,
I want to give you more.

THE FIRE

You lit a fire under my ass,
My ass cheeks were burned to a crisp,
I can't sit down anymore,
All that constructive criticism,
All that tough love,
It's paying off,
I get it now,
Thanks for lighting the match,
Slim chance I am going back to killing roaches now.

*When you are dealing with a real woman, she will check you when she feels you are slipping. Use the constructive criticism phellas.

IT'S ME

I'm the only man she wants,
We have real conversations,
While I drink Hennessy and she smokes her blunt,
I get to know her more every day,
I reciprocate the energy and tell her more about myself,
Lately I been all peeling layers off of my onion,
She loves my company,
She is cool with sitting in the house and chilling,
She covers her ass in public and rarely shows skin,
I love her modesty, its attractive,
Her smile brightens my day and it tells me I'm doing something right,
We argue often but loves brings us back together,
I'm in good hands,
I put in my application and she hired me,
I'm working for life,
Employee of the Lifetime.

THE WISE FARMER

I found some good soil,
No sticks, no rocks,
It's fertile and ready for crops,
I'm ready to plant my seeds here,
Ensure my existence into future generations,
I need to live on,
Life is short,
Everyday someone dies young,
Most die without life insurance,
Most have no kids to carry on their name,
Get to humping, Brother Brown,
What are you waiting on?

PS: Kids are expensive. I know.

ANTENNA LOVE

The mind is like a radio transmitter.
It's hard to get a clear station with all the frequencies (women) I am entertaining.
I'm getting static due to me trying to entertain all these stations at one time.
Talking to and interviewing all these different women has made me totally forget what station I was seeking in the first place.

What channel am I on?
I love the spark of the new energy,
I love the feeling of having options.
I am feeding the wrong wolf,
Asking myself,

Do I want a stay at home wife that cooks daily and takes care of the kids?
Do I want a wife that works hard and works long hours and makes money but, doesn't have energy to fuck me to relieve my tension?
Do I just want a small-brained bitch that fucks on command?

With these stations playing at once,
Honestly, I don't know what I'm looking for!

I AIR-BALLED

I play too much,
I never say too much,
I'm always laughing,
I'm always giggling,
I never shoot my shoot,
I'm always dribbling,
Trying to master this crossover is my excuse,
I got it down now,
It's time to shoot my shot,
I missed badly,
She said she was dating a few men,
She is only accepting applications for a friend,
I took too long,
Damn, I air-balled.

FIND A NEW ONE

I'm getting wiser and I'm losing friends,
Rest in peace to my attention span,
I'm zoning out when my girl vent to me,
Every now and then I chime in and say "That's Crazy" to keep her talking,
She gets mad when I'm no longer listening,
I have my own problems I am dealing with,
Her daily job gossip is redundant,
Every day is the same shit,
Quit that motherfucking Job!
Find a new one.

MY FIRST MURDER

What Happened to the Jamal that used to be your wingman?
What happened to Jamal that was guaranteed 10 numbers a night in the club?
What happened to the Jamal that used to juggle 5 women at a time and sell them the same dream?
What happened to the Jamal that was down to hit a "lick" no matter the risk?
What happened to the Jamal that was full of pride and always had to have his way?
What happened to the Jamal that used to steal thousands of dollars worth of clothes?
What happened to the Jamal that used to stay drunk and fall asleep in the club?
What happened to the Jamal that used to cheat on all his girlfriends?
I KILLED HIM!!!
I brutally murdered him,
I don't think he is coming back anymore,
I dismembered the body so good, no one can find the body,
So when you ask what happened to the old Jamal?
My answer is: He is dead,
I turned over a new leaf,
I went the legal route,
I have a girlfriend I plan on marrying now,
I have attainable goals I plan to manifest now,
Nothing can stop me now,
Clear Mind, Clear Grind,
How you like me now?

PS: For a man to truly live, part of him has to die or all of him has to die in attempt to be born again.

REALITY CHECK

We have to be our own critics and check ourselves from time to time. This mile is when I had to check Brother Brown.

REALITY CHECK! (LETTER TO MYSELF)

You tripping, dog,
You slipping, dog,
It's some shit on your mind, you need to get it off,
You thinking too much, and that's causing you to drink too much,
You fucking up bread you know you don't have,
You'll save more money masturbating, instead of chasing ass,
Those $40 dates adding up bro,
It's crazy how a chick can get a meal but when your mans want to hold something its "Fuck No",
The realest shit you ever wrote be the shit you never spoke,
You need to find yourself a good woman and start that empire,
Before you perish like outdated fruit,
Life gets shorter every step into the future,
You just seen Vince and an hour later, he died,
You are so comfortable with death, you don't even cry;

The Universe took him to tell you to wake the fuck up and complete them goals:

- Finish this book you writing
- Earn that PHD in remembrance of Dr. Kelso
- Travel the world
- Stay true to your Savings goals
-

You smart as hell, but you rather take your money to the streets,
You make more money in the streets than you do at work,
Shhhhhh... That's quiet money though!,

As for women, you have a few good candidates in your interview process:
- One is in Law School and will be successful in the long run.
- One has a beautiful personality and you enjoy her company.
- One is humble and down to earth. Goal oriented and driven.
- One is older. She can cook and she is solitude in the female form.

Keep Running...

You don't care about the salary of a woman,
You are a sapiosexual,
You are attracted to intelligence and the mind because the mind
will raise the child,
Money will simply provide material resources,
Time is ticking,
Beware of the grey hair,
Get your shit together before it's too late!

STILL?

Still tripping huh?
Still bitching huh?
You don't get it bruh!!
You are going to lose everything chasing nothing!
In this life you are you,
But you are nothing without a woman,
Raised by a single one, but cant seem to settle down
Just running around town being Brother Brown,
Time is ticking,
Stop tripping,
Stop Bitching,
Just listen to her when she venting,
Stop being dismissive,
Open your mind,
You been out here a long time Posting Relationship Openings,
Reviewing Resumes,
Interviewing Candidates,
One made it through,
She is worth it,
"DON'T FUCK THIS UP!!!"

Keep Running...

DUMMY (REALITY CHECK PART 2)

Still Tripping,
Still Bitchin,
You are on the verge of losing that woman,
Her love for you is diminishing,
You have the world in the palm of your hands,
Keep it up and it will slither through them like sand,
She will move on to another man,
You will see him enjoying her via Instagram,
Your boys will laugh at you and say, "Damn",
Tighten the fuck up,
You are still full of foolish pride,
You hurt her feelings and don't even apologize,
You don't console her when she is crying,
You have some fucking nerve,
This is your last reality check,
If you end up losing her, just know it was your fault,
You didn't deserve her to begin with,
Dummy!

HEARTBREAKS

Love is War.

Sometimes we win,

Sometimes we lose.

SHATTERED ILLUSIONS

I took you face value. I didn't do my homework. Every word you said I accepted as truth. I admit - I was blinded by your mind. Your mind and thoughts were more attractive than your physical features and believe me - that body banging!

Your standards are too high, and I am still in the process of becoming me. We head-butt often about what you call common sense. I am learning things now that I should have learned as a child. You get upset because of the process of my development. I don't blame you. Understand me though. I learn something new every day.

Growing up, I had no examples of the black family to use as a blueprint. I am accustomed to being alone. It is easy for me to leave you, and accept it if you do the same. Everything that I ever loved either left me or died. So being alone is my natural niche I inhabit.

My pride was a vice. It was also my defense mechanism. I lost my only weapon when I put it to the side. I am defenseless now as I pick up my heart in pieces off the floor. It's time to move on and try again. This cycle never stops. I think I am better off alone sometimes.

Who you portrayed yourself to be is totally different from who you are. What you say is not what you mean; it is just how you felt at the time. I understand that, and that is why I still call. I know you think about me even though you reject my calls and don't reply to my text messages.

You have too much pride instilled in you, but I know you are trying to protect yourself. I am not here to hurt you; I am just trying to love you. You don't know the affect you had on me. You left me at the drop of a dime. How? I'm still trying to understand. You told me you were rocking with me, but YOU determined that was a lie!

I'll give you a second chance, just promise you won't leave me out here scrambling again. Don't sell me dreams. I am cheap. I keep receipts. So, don't be surprised if I want my money back or my love. My marathon must continue. I will see you around...

Keep Running...

DAMAGED GOODS

Damn, I want to pick up the phone and call you,
but my pride is in the way,
Besides, if you do answer, I don't even know what I'm going to say
How are you? How is life? Is Everything everything?

Inside me lies instilled pride
In the back of my mind, I keep hope alive
that we will be together again;

I have beautiful women wanting to cuff me, but I just tell them just
suck me and fuck me,
I tell them don't trust me with their heart because I no longer have
one of my own,
It's still with you after all these years;

How can someone trust me with what I don't even have myself?
You made me heartless. Thanks.
Women fall into the abyss of my Venus flytrap
Because they think they can change my ways and win me over,
They lose themselves trying to find me,
The search for knowledge of self never ceases,
I love how relationships start but I hate how they end,
The sour taste in my mouth is flavorful,
Two years later and I still taste it,
The only way to get over you is to move on, but I'm over here
wondering what if?
I'm dipping and ducking relationships like Mayweather on them
ropes,
My next one will be my last one;

Temporary situations are a waste of time - Long-term success is the
mission,
I was good until you damaged me, and now, no one wants damaged
goods!

CHILL OUT

All I do is go to work at 6 am and get off at 2,
Grab some food and come back home to you,
I don't go out; I'm home with you all day,
How am I cheating?
I'm broke,
I don't even have a car,
Nobody wants my ass,
I'm surprised you still do,
I know you love me,
You need to chill out,
Unnecessary stress will be the death of this relationship,
I'm just being honest.

*When a man is trying to get right, the last thing he wants to hear is his woman complaining and nagging. He is already under enough stress.

I CAN'T TELL NOBODY

Listen.

See the truth is that I do like you; shit, I damn near love you. I envision us in the big house, with the nice cars, and children everywhere. Money saved, Bills Paid; shit, we straight. That's the relationship goals I want to manifest (fuck them celebrity couples as examples). You think I am weird, but you are still curious and want to know me. You ask me why I act the way I do and why I am all about you. Can I borrow your ear? Let me explain. I did a case study to see who would be happy to find out that ol' Brother Brown actually has a girl he likes. I am 0 for 6 so far.

I told my mother, and she tells me to take it slow because it is too early. But I like you now, and I want you now. She is entitled to her opinion, but my vision is still clear: I choose you.

I wish I could tell my pops, but I never met him. He would probably say some wild shit to alter my thoughts away from the vision. I want you.

I told my Grandmother, and she is all for it. She says, "She is a huge fan of that get together young and grow old love." That is reassurance to manifest my vision; I want you.

I told all my boys and they laughed at me. They said:

- "I don't want to hunt alone, bro."

- "You getting soft on me, bro."

- "Don't retire on me yet bro, I need a wingman."

- "You too young bro, we still got time to play."

- "Man, you tripping, you still have a few hoes you haven't hit yet."

- "You can have that long distance shit, I'm in my prime."

Keep Running...

Boys will be Boys, right?

When I feel down, you tell me to never give up and carry on.

Life is an obstacle course, you pace me on my marathon.

I share my deepest thoughts with you, you understand me.

Even though we just met, I love you like family.

Everyone I share my good news with doesn't care. I don't expect them to. But, the above statements are what are being sent in a stamped envelope to the universe on a daily basis. My positive letters might get lost in God's mail container. I keep hope alive. I am the cause to my effects. I am the ruler of my destiny.

When I am with you, I am unreasonably happy. My spirit meter is green. You fill my soul when we enter the Aleph. Ever wonder why I want to cuddle all day and waste a day laying there with you? You give me peace of mind. You make me feel good inside; you are an escape from reality in the physical form. Your presence is a present; A gift from heaven above.

I want to tell the world how I feel about you and set an example of love.

But negative people are like air; they are everywhere.

So, I talk to your picture when you don't answer the phone.

This poem can go on forever with the thoughts that pace my mind. I know I say the same thing over and over about how I feel about you. Want to know why? I CAN'T TELL NOBODY...

BUT YOU!

THE WIND

Blood in the form of teardrops,
Fall from her broken heart,
It's my entire fault,
Too many lies on my end,
She claimed I put her second to my friends,
They give me life,
You are not exciting,
Your arguments drain me,
They empty my soul,
I can't do this anymore,
The best decision for me is to leave,
I'm Gone,
Back in the wind I go.

GAMBLING

You always lose more than you win. If you win you are only making back money that was lost.

DICE GAME CHRONICLES

I ask the houseman is the pot right before I shoot my dice,
Its 8 shooters in here we gone be all night,
I put up in the pot, then I get my side bets right,
It's a sucker at every dice game,
But I'm no lollipop,
I shake my dice twice then let them drop,
4,5,6 is what the dice read,
Now I'm up $150 but that's light cheese,
Picking up my money I just smile and laugh,
I hear somebody ask, "Are we betting back?",
Yeah it's a bet,
I'm out there,
Make sure that pot right house.

JACKPOT

I walk up to the crap table and ask the players how it's looking?
They tell me I came at the right time,
I drop a $25 chip on the bonus bet,
I usually don't put my faith in other shooters but I'm optimistic tonight,
I kid you not; he rolled for about an hour,
And he hit all combinations for the bonus bet,
I made $5000 that night.

LOST IT ALL

The crap table was cold,
I should have took my losses and rolled,
But, no,
Still, I stood there,
Thinking the luck would change,
7 after 7,
Crap out after crap out,
At the end of that day,
I lost it all,
I couldn't even get food on the way home,
Let alone toll money,
Plus, I was in the middle week of the pay period,
Back to the infamous noodle diet.

WHEN GAMBLING, KNOW WHEN TO WALK AWAY!

FUCK A JOB

I hate working
I know I am not the first to admit it
I rather be chilling at home
Rubbing my feet together like a cricket
The workweeks are long
The weekends are short lived
No time for anything
My entire existence is scheduled around somewhere I don't want to be
This cannot be life
Whose idea was this?

Keep Running...

HE...

He had of dreams of being a cop, but the system stopped them,
He is one of the last ones alive from his block, how you ask? His friends were all slipping when the ops caught them.
He can't get a job in his field due to a charge.
He feels that he wasted 4 years on that degree,
He gets overwhelmed in interviews due to anxiety,
He feels less of a man because he girl has been paying the bills for the last 7 months.
He has trust issues due to deals going bad with his closest friends from childhood,
He drinks to escape the trauma, but lately has been using the pen to release his pain in attempt to save his liver,
He doesn't answer his phone anymore because he wants to talk to his soul and hear his inner voice only,
He contemplates suicide often, but patience is his superpower and he knows better days will soon come,
He is not happy with life, and therefore can care less about anyone else and how they feel;

He is going through a lot;

Who is he?
He is I,
I am he,
Brother Brown.

NO SHOVEL NEEDED

I told my cousin to get a job to take care of his son,
He said, "Fuck a Job, I am one!"
I am a hustler,
I supply demands of all customers,
I sell cold water in the heat,
I sell cheap sandals for your feet,
Around the 4th of July I even have the plug on meat,
I do what I have to do,
I understand that you went to school,
That's cool,
I'm not a fool,
Experience was my teacher,
I replied, "Damn I don't need a shovel to dig that!",
You right,
Fuck a Job.

ROYALTY

I'm applying for jobs I won't get,
I'm over qualified,
I am a descendant of kings,
No place of employment is worth my time or presence,
Entrepreneurship is the best route to take,
I evaluated myself,
I know my worth,
I have to get it,
The World is mine.

THE BIGGER PICTURE

Knowing is half the battle,
Working for the man, being treated like cattle,
Once my shift ends,
I look up and another cow walks in,
Ready to start where I left off,
This is checkers, nowhere near chess yall,
No thinking involved,
The work is redundant,
Time goes slowly,
No room for advancement,
I'll be damned if I work on this assembly line,
All my life and just die,
Fuck a 2-week notice,
I quit...
I have to get what I deserve.

I DIDN'T

I didn't quit,
I just changed my mind,
I had to switch up the hustle,
It's time to reinvent myself,
Something Bigger,
Something Better,
I would tell you my next move,
I spare doing so because I fear your opinions,
You might talk me out of my dreams,
It happened before,
They didn't seem interested and kept criticizing my idea,
You should do it this way,
Or
I don't see it popping Bro honestly,
I no longer seek validation from others,
What's gone be will be,
Every man walks his own path.

THOUGHTS FROM THE PLANTATION

Routine is a silent killer,
Ask anyone who works a 9 to 5,
Anything new and exciting is seductive to most proletariats,
One day you will get tired of,
Working for the man,
Helping him stay rich,
While scraping the crumbs from the pie,
You've been deprived a slice of,
Know why you are working and never be afraid to quit or switch
plantations!

DEUCES

My spirit is ashy,
I need some universal lotion,
Why you ask,
Because at my job I have to wait for someone to die to get a promotion,
The person in the position I desire is the same age as me,
I heard through the grapevine she is fucking the VP,
Should I wait?
Should I pray?
Should I leave?
Should I stay?
Looking down as step off this corporate ladder.

WATER BREAK

Thanks for making it thus far in the book. I hope you found some things that you can relate to. Can you do me a favor?

Take a picture and post this on your social media and let people know how good of a book it is or isn't.

- Call 3 of your closet friends and tell them to get this book.

- Email me at Jamalbrown3@gmail.com and give me some feedback. I will email you back.

- Follow me on social media:

  Instagram – "Brotherbrown856"

  Facebook – Like "BrotherBrown the Author"

Thanks in advance. Get back on the track and keep running with me. We have only 13 miles to go. You got this. Come on. Let's Go.

Remember,

Pace Yourself.

COLLEGE

College is one of the best experiences a person can experience. It is fun, but it is not cheap.

COLLEGE

Homework is assigned,
Read the opinion of an author,
Write your opinion on his or her views,
Then get a grade based on your opinion,
By the opinion of the professor,

Typing papers is a waste of time!

COST TOO MUCH

NO POEM NEEDED.

COLLEGE

IS

TOO

EXPENSIVE!

.

WHAT THE FUCK AM I DOING?

I am sitting in class on my ass. My pocket vibrates. Incoming text and picture from my favorite cousin that reads: Just bought the new Corvette for "70 thousand cash."

What the fuck am I doing?

I have over 30 books in my library, and I just met a girl who has over 60 in hers. She has a full ride to Law school and aspires to graduate top in her class and all I do is patrol a military base on the graveyard shift Monday through Thursday. She likes me and I like her but one question lingers in the back of my head.

What The fuck am I doing?

I am a victim of the paycheck-to-paycheck cycle and I know this when I am sober, but when that alcohol mixes with my soul I spend money like I have my bills paid 5 years in advance. After I wake up hung-over with a fast beating heart, I hesitate to log into my online bank account. After successful login and seeing the damage my alter ego caused, I tell myself "I could have paid a bill with that money", then go back to sleep and say "No more drinking"

What the fuck am I doing?

I am over here setting savings goals for myself: Save $10,000 by my birthday for a vacation. My man said he ready to spend $10,000 with me on some product but I am out the game. He told me he got $500 from 20 girls and he doesn't owe them back. Meanwhile I am on this date eating cheap just to impress this chick just so I can hit and add her to the list.

What the fuck am I doing?

My friend is the only one out of the crew that has a girlfriend. Shit we all had one at one time. Now I'm slaying hoes left and right and then kick them out of my sight. I roll dolo because I will never tell on myself. I know my bro faithful but these chicks' bad, as shit and I need a wingman. There was a time where I was Robin and he was Batman,

Keep Running...

I know that dog still resides in him. I know I am supposed to be checking him when he cheating because he will lose it if he lost her, but I could care less. I need someone to party with.

What the fuck am I doing?

Sat in on many panels and read many books, but still haven't took a step forward in any direction towards success. I can see the big picture clearly but the small steps make it seem impossible to reach via paperwork and politics. I want my money while I am young. They say take it slow and good things will come to those who wait, but with that mindset I will end up 76 in front of the liquor store telling the tale of "Freaknik" over and over while panhandling. Miss me with that bullshit. I daydream daily to escape reality, but when I come too, the question still remains:

What the fuck am I doing?

The answer is simple: I'm not doing anything; I am BULLSHITTING!

BEAT THE ODDS

Typing paper after paper,
Defending thesis after thesis,
This hill to graduation I've been climbing has been the steepest,
Searching within myself, I had to look the deepest,
I came to learn the ways of the working world,
I already mastered the streets,
Find a way or make one is the motto at this institution,
I've been applying the science to that logic all my life,
During my matriculation here at CAU,
I aced the midterms and passed the finals,
So when I received the email saying,
I am eligible to graduate,
I realized that I am no longer a statistic,
I am a black man with a degree,
I beat the odds,
At least I thought.

Tone and I at graduation from Clark Atlanta University. Class of 2015.

IS IT ENOUGH?

It's been 3 years since I graduated from a historically black college,
All I have to my name is knowledge,
I can't find a job so I have no dollars,
They told me life would be better with a college degree,
All my homies back home still stuck in the streets,
They are doing way better than me,
Damn,
Was I better off trapping?
Trapping in a trap,
While knowing it's a trap,
Go to prison,
Get out,
Then go straight back to the trap,
And risk going back to the pen,
Repeating the cycle all over again,
Will it ever end?
It only makes sense if it makes money,
All money aint good though,
I don't want to go to prison,
I'll just keep applying and waiting,
Something will fall through.

GROWING UP IN THE HOOD WE LEARN TO HUSTLE AND SURVIVE AT
AN EARLY AGE. SO, WHEN BILLS ARE STEADY ROLLING IN AND THE
JOBS ARE NOT CALLING BACK FAST ENOUGH, WHAT YOU THINK IS
THE NEXT STEP? STREETS ARE ALWAYS HIRING!

ALCOHOL

Have you ever tried to get drunk, but you couldn't because your thoughts were racing and sobering you up after each shot? It happens to me often. I guess the mind is powerful enough to think straight even when the presences of outside substances are in the body. We as people often seek temporarily relief from life and the obstacles that come with it. The mind will not let you alter off track for any reason. Even if you happen too, the thoughts will become heavy on your conscience and will be released in a rant or a vent session. This is why they say a drunken mouth speaks so much truth. Nothing can be bottled forever. Talk to your closest friends or write it down. Either way, FREE THE DEMONS!!

LEAVE ME A MESSAGE

I'm drinking Hennessy straight,
I don't chase it any more,
Life is too much,
I can't take it any more,
I tried to fast from alcohol,
Shit didn't last long,
I kept hanging up on it,
Bitch kept calling me back,
Even left a few messages,
Eventually I answered,
Now I'm staring at the bottom of the bottle,
Here we go again,
Will I ever stop drinking?

HENNESSY TALKS

Pop my seal,
Open me up,
Put your lips on mine,
Swallow my venom,
Pour me on the graves of all your friends that died,
Take me to the block with you,
Let your homies pass me around,
Treat me like my cousin "Blunt",
Take me with you to see that chick later,
Let me do the talking,
Once I enter her veins, She is bound to loosen up,
You will know when she starts venting,
That's where you come in,
Take it from here,
Thank me later for the extra stamina I instilled in you,
You know you be "Nutting early",
I apologize for the hangover in advance,

Every man in America has gotten drunk or a little buzzed prior to
having sex before. It is universal. It enhances our performance. At
least, we think it does.

I WANT TO LIVE

I was chugging on that glass bottle,
Drinking all my pain away,
It was an accident on the highway to my expressions,
I can't fathom anything to say,
I don't know what's going on with me,
Everyone keeps asking what's wrong with me,
I can't put it in words,
I'm just down,
I can't elaborate on how I am feeling,
I'm pushing everyone away, but pulling that bottle closer,
It's crazy how no human ever will, but a substance will truly know you,
It's always there for you,
It's always willing to care of you,
You can even bring a friend, that substance gone share with you,
You can even vent to it, the bottle don't judge,
It won't even say a word,
All it requires is a hug,
A hug from your hands to wrap around the neck of the bottle,
Keep Drinking Nigga,
Deep Thinking Nigga,
Its water in your boat Captain, Keep Sinking Nigga,
My advice to you is: Drop that bottle on the ground and shatter the glass,
Get off your ass, Get Mad, and get some Cash,
You hear the bottle saying: "Fuck Your Liver",
Reply: "Nah Fuck You Nigga",
I WANT TO LIVE!!!

I wrote this poem drunk, pondering life and wondering why I do what I do to cope with depression and stress as a black man in America. We need more options and outlets to deal with stress and depression. Alcohol and other drugs are temporary relief that serves as a short-term escape from realty into the sunken place. I suggest you seek

Keep Running...   136

counseling or start a journal and just jot down thoughts and feelings from time to time in attempt to cease bottling up emotions. It's hard for us men to communicate how we feel these days due to the possibility that we may be seen weak or soft. Majority of the people judging you don't know you. Get your life in order on an individual level. All else is obsolete. Silence the critics.

STILL I DROWN

Losing love for things I once enjoyed,
Depression is real; it stole my joy,
Nothing compares to how things were back in the day,
Occasionally, I drink in attempt to eliminate the madness,
It's a revolving door that is always open,
Drink Heavy,
Act Crazy,
Tell Myself "Never Again",
Then end up drinking again,
I need to jump off this hamster wheel,
And walk towards the light,

After a heavy night of drinking, we have all said the following phrase:
"Man I am not drinking anymore, I am done with alcohol." LOL.

SWIMMING IN HENNESSEY

Heavy Drinking,
Deep thinking,
My ship sinking,
No foundation or anchor,
Thoughts and emotions are sailing everywhere,
Some days, I want to just hustle pills, and scam bank accounts,
Somedays, I want to take this five, grand, and skip the country forever,
Some days, I want to get a PHD and become a psychologist,
But today, I want to drop some knowledge.
I'm from the hood and I graduated college
With a 3.0, so I guess I am a scholar
Mother raised me, I never met my Father,
With a focused grind, anything can be accomplished,
　　　At least that is what I thought....

I got the degree, but no Job
What did I learn? What do I know? How can I use it?
If you have education, with no experience, you are fucking useless!
I should have picked up a trade; there, is no money in the classroom...

Swimming in my thoughts, drowning in my feelings,
Sky is the Limit, I can't seem to see past the ceiling,
When, the Hennessey mix with my soul, the truth is born,
Thoughts run smoothly, and my sword (tongue) is sharpened,
If I can feel this way permanently, it will be a super power,
I can talk my way into and out of anything,
　　　I can either, talk shit or talk slick,
　　　I feel my powers are wearing off,
　　　Pour me up!

Keep Running...   139

THE NEXT LEVEL

Thinking and Drinking,
Drinking and Thinking,
Simultaneously planning my next move,
It has to be a chess move,
Checkers logic wont help at this level,
Everyone is playing to win here,
Love don't live here,
Leave them emotions at the door,
Learn and apply,
Or Die.

Everything you have been through is preparing you for the next level but remember this: Nobody cares about you been through; they only care about how you persevered and made it through! People want to apply your formula to escape their problems, not compare and contrast them.

DRUGS

Drugs plague the black community on a daily basis. It has been for years. I've had my experiences with them. These are my tales....

DO YOU KNOW A DRUG ADDICT?

Finding empty pens in random places throughout the house,
The scent of burnt plastic is present,
Thinking to myself "I needed them pens for school",
What are you using them for?
Why is your jaw moving like that when you talk?
What's up with the glare in your eyes?
Why you keep moving?
Can you stay still?
Why you scratch your head every 5 minutes?
You don't even have to answer that,
I already know,
You are getting high,
Damn,
Never thought you would ride that white horse,
You don't even like animals,
If this gets out to my friends,
Just expect to hear about a few fights,
I might get suspended for defending you and myself,
I hope you can shake it,
I love you,
I'm too scared to check you,
Even though I know you are slowly killing yourself,
I'll never say anything to you,
This poem is my plea.

I'M HIGH

After a few deep pulls, everything slowed down,
Talking to myself like,
"Whoa Now",
I'm moving slow but my thoughts are sharp,
I'm so high I can hear my heart,
I kick a freestyle over the acapella, and laugh to myself,
Then glance at some snacks on the shelf,
My mouth is dry,
My stomach is howling,
I guess this is what "having the munchies" feels like,
Took me damn near 3 minutes to open a honey bun,
After the short fight with the plastic, I took a bite,
Motherfucking honey bun never tasted this good,
Why are simplest things suddenly so funny?
I like this feeling, I can get used to this.

Everything tastes a million times better when you are high.

THE DAY PERKY CALLED

Incoming call from an unknown number,
Ayo – who is this,
It's me perky, what's up with you?
I don't fuck with you anymore, bro,
Perky told me the truth, he said,
I know you miss me in your system,
I can tell by the way you are scratching and itching,
You miss me?
I miss you,
I miss being in control of your soul,
Dictating your thoughts and actions,
Let me ease you, you are jittery,
Let's go to Cloud 9,
One more time wouldn't hurt.
Would it?
I guess not.

MILITARY

Be all that you can be. I served the country for a few years. These are the tales.

WAVE KING

If I take my wave cap off you might throw up,
My waves spinning,
I am the wave king,
I put no products in my hair,
It just grows like that,
To answer your questions,
To spare you throwing up on me,
I'm keeping my hat on.

This is proof I am the Wave King!

MR. CLEAN

Barber sat me in the chair,
Three minutes later,
I had no hair,
I looked in the mirror and couldn't believe it,
Damn, I look like a kneecap,
A whole peanut,
Better yet a thumb.

Me with a baldhead during basic training for the army

LETTER TO SAM

People often ask me why I joined the Army,
They expect me to say, "To serve the country,"
But Honestly,
I joined for college money,
I graduated with my Bachelors,
Then seen that tab for 60k,
From Sallie Mae,
And said fuck my Masters,
While serving in the army all I did was pump gas,
Civilians thank me for my service,
Out of uniform white women see me and grip their purses,
Oxymoron ass humans,
Thinking back on my decision to join,
I don't regret it,
I would do it again and not think twice,
I met some cool people,
And get $136 per month for the rest of my life,
Fuck the V.A.

AMERICA ATE ITS BABY

Dear America,

You sold me on a half-truth,
I took it face value,
I didn't read the fine print,
Now I'm seeking the truth,
On this quest back to refinement,
Since you served us let us serve you,
That's what jobs say,
Veterans get hired first around here,
My employment detector determined that was a lie,
Why y'all haven't hire me quickly as advertised,
Why not hire me on the spot?
Fuck them qualifications, why post them,
Knowing the company will train me up to standard when hired,
The world was hungry,
America ate its baby,
Don't be surprised when you see me in your bushes,
Trying to take from you what the world deprived me of,

Sincerely,

An Angry Vet.

I'M COMING BACK

Life is rough for a recently separated veteran,
No jobs hiring,
Bills rolling in constantly like waves hitting the shoreline,
Depression and Stress settling in,
Everyone is constantly asking what is my next move,
They say it should be easy for me to find a job,
Based on all the training I went through,
Shit I said the same thing,
But still my application goes unseen when I apply,
I'm just waiting,
Fuck this shit,
Tell Uncle Sam I am coming back,
I can't win,
No love for a civilian out here,
Off with the beard.

Me with a beard before I had to cut it off for the army

CRIME & JAIL

I wish jail on no man
It is a waste of time
Mistakes are made to learn from
But in this system, you might get lost
And never given a second chance to right your wrongs
Time is not worth the time.

DUI

Dosing in and out of consciousness,
Drinking and Driving,
Driving and Drinking,
My thoughts weren't calculated, I wasn't thinking,
6 years later, I can still hear her cries,
That woman that I crashed into almost died,
I could've been charged with vehicular homicide,
And sentenced to 25,
Fate wasn't dealt in my cards,
I am living my second chance at life,
That is why I go so hard,
I wasn't supposed to be here,
I cherish every moment.

CONCRETE COUCH

Sitting on this concrete couch,
Pondering what life is all about,
Surrounded by sexually frustrated tough guys,
Who lust for some ass, but I'll be damned if they touch mine,
I haven't seen the Sun in a few days; it's starting to fuck with me,
I get one phone call per day, but nobody accepts the charges,
While incarcerated I feel forgotten,
I held my dreams at gunpoint, then shot them,
I can only blame the man in the mirror,
To pass the time I meditate on better days to see my future clearer.
It's time to go to court now.

I'm shackled and chained to a bench,
Mumbling to myself "This is nothing but the workings of Willie Lynch",
The judge comes out in his superhero robe,
He looks right through me like glass;
Better yet – bottled water,
Then asks, "Are you aware of the charges Brother Brown?".

"Yes, your honor. I am".

At this moment my stomach hurting and my soul nervous talking to
myself saying:

- I hope the judge feeling good today,
- I hope his wife hasn't pissed him off lately,
- I hope he got some ass last night!

Why court is always scheduled on Monday?

The one-day of the week all proletariats oppose their existence,

Snapping out of my daze as the judge clears his throats to sentence
me.

Keep Running...   156

To my surprise he says:

"Brother Brown, I am going to let you go today and I never want to see you in my courtroom again, take this as a blessing",

"Thank you, your honor, you won't see me again!!!"

THE JAILHOUSE LAWYER

You committed every crime,
You learned every law,
You know the disposition for each case before the judge bangs his
gavel,
You know the exact amount of time for any crime,
You seem to have all the answers,
I have a question,
If you know all this, why the hell are you in here with me?
Why aren't you a lawyer?
Why aren't you a Judge?
Why aren't you a DA?
Why aren't you a Prosecutor?

Wasted Talent if you ask me!

Repeat offenders become experts when it comes to crimes and how
the process goes. It is the Funniest thing ever. For the readers who
have been locked up before, you know what I mean.

LIFE OF A BOOSTER

I walk in the store and flirt with the greeter,
What's up I'm Brother Brown I am honored to meet you,
Can you please direct me to the designer shit?
So, I can steal,
I can't afford to buy it,
I didn't say that, but I was thinking it,
Let me get back to the story,
It's a demand for expensive clothes,
I must supply the needs of the streets,
So, I grab the highest priced items so I can sell them for half,
10 shirts at $500 a piece, you do the math,
One of my clients paid me upfront,
So, I have to get it,
That "I came up short shit",
They aren't trying to hear it,
All the garments I took are tucked and secured,
You wouldn't know I had on 5 shirts and 5 stashed,
Time to get out of here,
My spider senses are tingling,
I sense someone is watching me,
Time to think quick, let me fake a phone call,
Talking to myself as I make my escape out the store,
This shit too easy,
Tomorrow, I will be back for more.

DON'T ADD UP

Crime is not worth the time,
It's a waste of,
Seconds,
Minutes,
Hours,
White man handing out life for that pile of powder,
He handing out years for them pounds of trees,
When you get out he put you on probation for another three,
Now you labeled a felon,
The newest victim to this system,
All because you was hustling backwards,
Basically, fishing with chicken,
Next time take a step back,
Analyze it from a higher plane,
Do the Math,
Make sure it adds up.

THE INDICTMENT

I got indicted,
I'm trying to fight it,
My anxiety is at its all-time highest,
I can't eat,
I can't sleep,
I left court a few hours ago,
I can still feel the cuffs on my hands and feet,
The tab for the lawyer is 20k,
There is no way around it,
This whole situation is astounding,
Moms depleted her account for the retainer,
Now the tab is 15,000,
5,000 a month for the next three months,
In my heart I know we can't afford it,
Why am I wasting this lawyer's time?
I'm considering taking my chances with a public defender,
If I lose trial and end up doing time,
It is all good,
I hear prison is where the greatest minds meet,
I'll be sure to come out sharp as a tack,
Armed with new information and a new game plan,
To ensure success for the remainder of my marathon,
Whatever is left of it.

SHAMELESS

My mother looks on as
I enter the courtroom,
Shackled and chained,
I can't remove the image from my brain,
She looked ashamed;

If she wasn't,
I was ashamed for her,
I was ashamed to be her son and causing her this unnecessary
stress,
Ashamed that I tarnished the family name,
Ashamed that I didn't live up to the expectations,
Ashamed that she accepted the fact that I was "the problem child",
Ashamed that I could never "Get Right",
Ashamed that I couldn't give her a return on her investment;

Life is funny
With
The ups and downs,
The twists and turns,
Make a change
For the better,
Do not wait until it's too late,
Don't be like me.

Keep Running...

IN ARMS' REACH

I hate being on probation,
I'm tired of checking in with my location,
They want to know everything,
From the size of my dick,
To the size of my wedding ring,
I'm not even married,
I'm single when I file my taxes,
I have a girlfriend though,
Back to my thoughts on probation,
This is the newest form of slavery huh?
I have to ask to leave the state,
I have to take a drug test every other day,
I am required to stay away from police and avoid interaction,
One slip up is all it takes,
For me to be back behind them gates,
No matter where I am,
I am always in arm's reach of a jail cell,
Is this America?
This Is America!

MAN UP

Probation Officer has to come to my crib,
Inspect where I live,
Family keeps calling me,
Asking me what I did,
It's none of their business though,
I do what I have to do to get the dough,
As long as I profit,
My actions are justified,
I don't need a lecture,
Take your two cents and throw them a change bucket,
I've already beat myself up about this situation,
I got myself in it,
I will get myself out of it,
In the meantime between time,
Do me a favor,
Love me through this,
That is all the support I need,
Thanks in advance.

FUCK THAT

I'll be damned,
If I take the stand,
And point out that man,
In exchange for a lesser sentence,
I don't mind doing the time,
So whatever you sentence me to,
I will figure it out when I get out,
Do as you please your honor,
I'm not snitching,
Fuck that.

DEPRESSION

Depression is real. Depression is like a mental chain on your brain. I pray that you find the key and liberate your mind. The following laps are my experiences and how I overcame them.

ROCK BOTTOM

I've reached rock bottom,
Its lonely here, population of exactly 3 people,
Just Me, Myself, and I,
Talking to myself because I am my own consultant,
Every piece of advice I get, I've already told myself,
I need new angles of perception to analyze from,
Without them, I am just reaffirming the failing self-fulfilling
prophecy,
Lord send me a sign,
It's so dark in here,
I cannot see anything,
Not even the palm of my hand,
The "light" is inside me; I just need to find the switch,
From rock bottom and its lowest pits,
There is only way to go,
Up.

When you get back on your feet, remember:
- You are no stranger to the struggle.
- Remain humble, you can fall off as quick as you got on.
- Always show love, always be grateful.

Remember this feeling and make a vow to never feel like this again.

WRITER'S BLOCK

I hear leaves rustling as I gaze out my office window,
Cars whiz by sounding like bullets cutting through air,
Warm wine rest on the desk,
Soft jazz instrumentals fill the atmosphere,
I'm at peace,
Euphoria is the feeling,
Finally,
I can start writing.

STILL I RUN

I'm tired of being strong; I need to be weak for a minute,
I need to meditate on better days,
Just think for a minute,
I have to find a better way,
All my old ones aren't working,
Daily I fall short of the lord's glory,
Nobody is Perfect,
But I'm trying,
I'm striving,
Honestly, I am barely surviving,
Sometimes I sit in a daze and just lose myself,
Sometimes I want to say fuck the world and shoot myself,
The only thing stopping me is I know that somebody needs my help,
I have to change my ways,
I have a soul to save,
Saving them will save me,
I am not alone in this fight,
My marathon continues...
Pace Yourself.

STRESS

I don't stress out, I poke my chest out.

-Nipsey Hussle

WHY?

Eyes closed with my head to the sky,
While meditating on one question,
Why?
So many answers to a one-word question,
What's your why?
Why do you do what you do?

TEARS

Fall from my face as I gaze into the sky,
I'm asking the lord why,
Why am I still here on earth?
What is the hold up?
I'm ready to come home father,
Free my soul from this prison made of flesh,
Mental chains plague my brain,
No keys around,
I'm tired of fighting,
I give up,
Take me Lord,
I'm ready to come.

SOMETIMES

Sometimes I look at my phone and just let it ring,
- I don't feel like talking at the moment.
- I could care less bout the new tea you recently obtained.
- I genuinely just don't care to be honest.

Sometimes my thoughts flow but I can't write anything,
- Writers block is real.
- I just sit there and stare at the computer screen.
- Music helps formulate thoughts sometimes.

Sometimes I drink myself into submission,
- I have to stop because I am an angry drunk.
- Hangovers are to gruesome the next day.
- I'm killing my liver.

Sometimes I want to go on a speaking fast,
- But my girl will constantly ask me what's wrong.
- She wants to solve every problem I have like my mother.
- We end up arguing for nothing.

Sometimes I want to drop everything and just leave,
- I just want to take about $4,000 and just go far away.
- I just want to throw my phone in the river so nobody can reach me to try to change my mind.
- I just want to just start from scratch and follow my intuition and live life on my terms.

Sometimes I go to places and just cry,
- I contemplate suicide often but my superpower which is patience keeps me postponing the action.
- Life is too much at times and people don't want to help; they just want to know what's going on so they can tell others. My current state of mind is not TEA!
- Death has to be easier than living. Maybe that's why when people die we say, "He is finally at peace". Life is turmoil.

These thoughts are not all the time – just SOMETIMES!

I CAN'T SLEEP

Laying in my bed,
Both hands behind my head,
Just staring at the popcorn ceiling,
My eyes are in sync with the blades from the ceiling fan,
As the blades turn, so do my eyes,
After mimicking them go in circles a few times,
I grow dizzy and blink,
Take a sip of water,
Then take a deep breath,
It's raining pretty hard outside,
My dog is snoring loud,
My girl steady tossing and turning,
I'm just up for no reason,
Nothing on TV,
SportsCenter showing the same highlights,
I hate when I can't sleep,
I'm a just lay here with my eyes closed,
Maybe that will work.

PRESSURE

Is on,
Expectations placed upon me,
Deadlines Approaching,
Questions asked but none answered,
I'm pushing everyone away,
I don't want help,
Let me think this through alone,
I will get back to you,
Don't be upset when I don't take your opinions into consideration,
I have to do what I feel is right for me,
A man has to do what a man has to do,

SOMEBODY

Save me,
I'm going crazy,
I haven't left the house in days,
I am a prisoner in my own crib,
Even though I have the keys to freedom,
I don't leave,
Where am I going?,
I have no job; I have nowhere to be,
I'm still waiting on a phone call from a plantation,
So, I type and chill,
Write poems that illustrate my dark side,
To help you better understand,
When I vent, people say, "You'll be alright",

Shit I tell myself that every night,
That's why I stay quiet when you ask me "What's wrong?",
You wouldn't understand!

Have you ever considered suicide but backed out last minute? You
are not alone. I did. Well I'm glad you are still here with us to. I'm here
to tell you that we all have a purpose and that purpose will present
itself when you least expect it. If you are currently considering
suicide please don't.

Nipsey Hussle states on Face the World:
Don't pull the trigger,
I feel like I got to tell you,
You got something to contribute,
Regardless of what you into,
Regardless of what you been through,
I feel like I got to tell you,
You got something to contribute,
.Find what you have to contribute to society. Leave a legacy.

RELIGION

"Bow your heads folks, these are praying times. The preacher man
been running that line more than the cable guy" -Loaded Lux.

WHAT'S THE HOLD UP?

I hear people saying God is coming back,
My question is where he at?
Where did he go?
People reply they don't know,
The 5 Percenters say they are the true and living Gods,
They great me in peace,
They show and prove all allegations to cease all doubt,
Most people don't agree with this thinking though,
They say God is coming when you least expect it,
Or after a great tragedy on earth,
Wasn't slavery tragic enough?
What about hurricane Katrina?
What about police brutality and the innocent killing of Black men?
What about the tsunamis?
What about these school shootings?
What about the organs of Africans being sold on the black market?

What else has to happen for God to say, "Ok, that's it. I am coming back?"

Seriously what is the hold up?

STORY TIME

Gather round....

VEGAS

I took a trip to Las Vegas. I met a girl there named Erika. After the exchange of names I conveyed to her that I was in the process of writing this book. She was an avid reader. I emailed her a sample to read. She gave her honest feedback and told me to keep her updated on the release upon completion. She was intrigued by what she read and wanted to support. I thanked her in advance and continued to enjoy my vacation. A few days later she reached out to me and said that she had to show me something. I inquired about what was to be showed to me. She instructed me to check my text messages. She sent me a picture of her latest tattoo. I was shocked to discover that the words quoted across her stomach where the exact ones from the introduction to this book (See Page 7). At that moment I knew my book was going to impact many people and that gave me all the motivation and determination I needed to finish this book.

Picture of the tattoo from Erika

Meeting Supreme Understanding
(Application of Knowledge)

After reading *How to Hustle and Win*, I reached out to the author. I found him on Facebook and contacted him. He responded and the rest is history. The knowledge he shared with me in person was in tune with what he was expressing in his book. I instantly had a mentor. One day as we sat around building I expressed to him that I was low on funds and asked did he know any ways to make some immediate cash.

He replied, yes, he needed help with a moving job. He had a budget of $200. He instructed me to go to Home Depot and get some extra hands to help. I was instructed to tell them that the job would last 2 hours and each person would be compensated $50. I found two guys and brought them to move site. After the job was completed, he paid the two guys $60 a piece. He gave me $80. He gave me more due to me handling all the logistics of the job. He said, "Money isn't hard to make, just use your brain." I nodded and went on about my day as I left the site of the job. From that two-hour job I learned knowledge and wisdom that could be used to make money in any situation.

True Story: A few months later a friend of mine reached out to me and asked if I knew anyone with a moving company. I told him I had one. It worked in my favor because he already had the trucks so that was one less problem I had to worry about. All I was tasked with was finding some cheap labor and putting the formula Supreme taught me into action. The client needed his whole house moved along with two full storage units. His initial offer was $1000. From hustler to hustler I knew he had more money, I just had to negotiate to get what I wanted. We agreed on $1200. On the day of the moving job I went back to that same Home Depot and found some cheap labor as instructed. The verbal contract was an all day moving job and after completion they will be paid $150 per person. So in total it was five including me. The move went smooth, and at the end of the job, I was given the $1200. I went and paid each worker $150 and kept $600 to myself. That's how you apply the science of the hustle and work from the neck up. This here is a thinking man game!

WHATEVER INFORMATION YOU OBTAIN, USE IT TO THE BEST OF YOUR ABILITY. USE THAT INFORMATION TO MAKE MONEY.

FAILURES

If in my quest 2 achieve my goals,
I stumble or crumble and lose my soul,
Those that knew me would easily co-sign,
There was never a life as hard as mine,
No father - no money - no chance and no guide,
I only follow my voice inside,
If it guides me wrong and I do not win,
I'll learn from mistakes and try 2 achieve again.

-Tupac Shakur

We all fall short when we strive for greatness. I am no stranger to the struggle. This mile contains all the failures I've endured on my marathon.

- I've failed the TSA Exam two times.
- I've failed the Customs and Border Protection Entrance Exam on the first go around. The second time around I passed it.
- In high school, I was late 32 times in one semester and had to repeat all the same classes. I ended up in the same class with my little brother and I was ineligible to play basketball the first half of my sophomore season.
- I wasn't chosen to study abroad while at Clark Atlanta University.
- I was fired from UPS. I wasn't aware until I tried to clock in.
- I have over 150 emails saying I wasn't qualified for the job and they are moving forward with another candidate.
- I've been denied phone numbers in the club.
- I've been told to my face that I received a job, only to receive a letter in the mail stating otherwise.
- I've lost 5k in Vegas and had to borrow money to get home.
- I've failed a shooting test in Kuwait when I was a contractor. If I had passed, I would've been making 90k annually.
- One Christmas I didn't buy anyone a gift. I only had bill money.
- In the year 2018, I only worked three months. That was rough year.
- I was 26 with a college degree working for $8 an hour (Very humbling).

DURING THESE FAILURES, I'VE LEARNED PRICELESS LESSONS. LOOKING BACK, I AM GLAD I FAILED.

DREAMS & GOALS

"Yeah I got dreams" (Crazy Legs Voice). Seriously though all dreams start off on paper. Write them down and create small goals and strive to achieve them.

Life is short. Before I meet my demise, I would like to meet a few people before it's my time to go. The list is as follows:

- Nipsey Hussle
- AZ
- J Cole
- Big Krit
- Mos Def
- President Obama
- Jadakiss
- Dave East
- Oprah Winfrey
- MAINO
- Mike Epps
- Kendrick Lamar
- Fabolous
- Wallo267 & Gillie Da Kid
- Master P
- Daymond John
- Denzel Washington
- Casanova 2x
- Lebron James
- Pimpin' Ken
- Tyler Perry
- Nas
- Jay Z
- Snoop Dogg
- Diddy
- Currensy
- Will Smith
- Styles P
- Swizz Beats
- Steve Harvey
- Kevin Hart
- Scarface
- Cozz
- Jamal Crawford
- Colin Kaepernick
- Dame Dash
- Milton Howery
- Hill Harper
- Floyd Mayweather
- Jonah Berger
- Meek Mill
- The Breakfast Club

This list may seem farfetched, but it is realistic. Hopefully you the reader can help me pull some strings and connect me with them. Dreams do come true. I'm hopeful to meet the individuals on the list on my marathon eventually. I just want to build with them and sharpen my sword.

- My goal is to sell over a million copies of this book and reach people all over the world.

- My goal is to become an international best-selling author and tour the world telling my story and doing pop up shops selling books and merchandise.

Other Goals:

1.Take a picture with Nas toasting champagne. The caption under the picture will read "Put your glass high if you made it out the stash spot and you are here to tell your story".

2. I want to receive an "All Money In" chain from Nipsey Hussle and become an honorary member of the Marathon team.

3. I want to play Meek Mill in HORSE for $1000. I will beat him easily.

4. I want to smoke a blunt with Snoop Dogg. He is the godfather of marijuana.

5. Interview Master P and thank him for his work and contributions to the culture.

6. Sit in on a studio session with Nipsey Hussle.

7.Shake LeBron's hand and thank him for his contribution to the culture and the NBA.

AS LONG AS I PACE MYSELF I WILL GET THERE.

DEATH

We all die in the end
Life is short
For some it's long
Live your life on your terms
Fuck the world
Fuck the critics
Live
Don't just exist.

I want to use this page to say RIP to all the friends and family I lost on my marathon thus far. I miss you all, and just know you will never be forgotten.

- Lil Tru
- Big Mike
- Jerome Chestnut
- Ms. Jenny
- VT
- Uncle Tony
- Goon
- Lil-Man
- Rocks
- Pedro
- Brianna Ford
- J-Mac
- Dr. Kelso
- Dre
- Harlem
- Willie Peed
- E-Dub

- Veez
- Malcolm X
- Tupac
- Aunt Ernie
- Vince
- David Sapp
- Double Take
- Erickeem
- SPC Harris (E4 Mafia)
- Killa Priest
- Ms. Dot
- Rick Dawkins
- Big Mike
- Cousin Mitchell
- Lil Man
- Tyrone
- Everyone that passed before their time

I SEE DEAD PEOPLE

They killed my Uncle Tony in the club,
He was out having a good time,

They killed my cousin "Dre" up the street from my house,
That changed the neighborhood,

Lil' Man died on the four-wheeler,
That's the reason I don't ride bikes,

They killed Rocks in the villas,
The news killed his grandmother,

They killed Jerome Chestnut,
He could sing his ass off,

Ms. Jenny died in Glen Park,
She was the candy lady,

Lil Tru was killed in his driveway,
His daughter was in the backseat,

Willie Peed died in Glen Park,
He was cool when he wasn't drinking,

Floyd died in Glen Park,
He dressed pretty smooth,

They stabbed Goon in a fight,
We went to Buckshutem together,

They killed E-Dub at a kick back,
He was from the neighborhood,

They killed Harlem,

Keep Running...   192

He was the funniest dude I knew,

They killed David Sapp; he was trying to run
He could jump out the gym (literally),

They killed Vince after a Party,
He threw up on me a few hours before he died,

They killed Lil Walt in his house in front of his kids,
Why couldn't they just take the money, and let him live?

Briana Ford died in a car accident,
She was beautiful,

Dr. Kelso had a heart attack,
He taught me a lot about life,

Cousin Rick Dawkins died in a car accident,
He had a way with words,

J-Mac died on the motorcycle,
He had on white loafers when I met him,

Veez was killed in the car,
He was too cool for school,

They found Tyrone body in the middle of the night,
He taught me a lot about life,

They killed SPC Harris on the basketball court,
We served in the army together.

They killed "Andre Harris' because he won the fight
Put them guns down,

They tried to kill my dreams of finishing this book
And become an author,

Keep Running...

They didn't know that the most powerful force
Is a focused grind,
Nothing can get in the way of what God has for me,
It was my destiny to finish this book.

I did it!

'

LONG LIVE TRU

Walking up to the casket to see you for the last time. Many thoughts run through my biscuit. As I get closer to the casket my heart drops as if I am on a rollercoaster. The sound of cries and screams roar throughout the church. The feeling of reassurance comforts me. You were loved!

I take two shots of my spit as I look at your lifeless body in the casket. I'm trying to hold back the tears, but a few snuck out. I taste them as I lick my lips. Funny memories rush to my mind. I laugh to myself.

Seeing your Mom cry over your body hit my soul. I felt her pain. When I got a chance to get close to her all I could do was hug her. Words wouldn't have done any justice. I miss you bro!

Seeing your Father break down and cry over you hit my spirit. You were loved by all. We feel empty without you around. The town will never will never be the same without you pacing the block, hooping at the park, and making us laugh in the barbershop.

They say death has to be easy because life is hard, but I rather struggle with you in person rather than take the easy way out. Struggle builds character and we were learning so much on our quest to become men.

You left a daughter behind. Sad thing is that she doesn't know what is going on yet. I pray the city doesn't get her like it does most girls. I have hope for her. When she asks me to tell her about you I don't know where I am going to start. To this day I think about you in the dark.

My hand shook as I reached over to drop the flower on your casket. Sniffles and cries cloud the atmosphere still. All that life you had to live, and that sucker took you out. It's not fair, but in this thing called life I don't make the rules.

When they buried you in the grave, they rushed to cover you in that dirt. I can't believe this is happening. I'm speechless as me and your closest friends cry our last tears around your burial site. We were

Keep Running...

the last ones there with you. Death couldn't even do us part. It's LONG LIVE TRU for eternity.

Your name lives on through funny memories and stories many of us have. There are too many to recall. From them Glen Park days to you visiting me in Atlanta. You have a section in my scrapbook because the love is real. You hold a special place in my heart. We are missing you out here. Now, all we can do is tell the tale of "Lil Tru". RIP Bro. I will see you when they get me.

At "Lil Tru" funeral looking on as they lower him into his final resting place.

LETTER TO LIL' WALT (NEPHEW)

You were too fly for your own kind,
That's why your wings were clipped,
I am saddened by your death,
One of my favorite cousins,
Gone too soon,
To forever live in the wind,
You ran a hell of a marathon,
I am honored for the miles we ran,
But,
This is where your marathon ends,
I will pace myself as I continue on,
I Love you cousin,
Everything about you,
They couldn't fuck with you,
They had to kill you,
Broke Ass Niggas,
Haters,
Fucking Cowards,
I hope they,
Die,
Slow,

THINKING OF YOU

I miss my cousin,
I never told him that I loved him,
I always shook his hands when I saw him,
I never hugged him,
Now he is gone,
Permanently a resident in the wind,
One day I will see him again,
I feel his spirit when the wind blows,
I know he is with me,
I am getting him tatted on me,
I am taking him wherever I go,
R.I.P Lil' Walt.

Keep Running...   199

R.I.P. Lil' Walt. Gone but never forgotten.

I'M DESENSITIZED...

Just got a call from the hood,
A childhood friend just died,
I took a deep breath and just shook my head,
I couldn't even cry,
Seeing so much death on this marathon,
I've grown accustomed to it,
We all die in the end,
I'm thankful for the times we shared; you were a true friend,
See you when I get there.

WHAT'S FREE?

Watching kids cry over the casket of their slain father,
The mother cries as she holds them up,
Close friends share memories during their speeches,
An old lady sings a song to cheer up the congregation,
At the repast swishers are broken down,
Blunts are rolled up,
Hennessy is poured on the concrete stone,
With the name of the deceased on it,
The next day, reality sets in,
Life Goes On,
I've seen this episode too many times,
Even though I hate this show,
I keep watching,
I will never miss a funeral,
I will always pay my respect.

IT'S NEVER GOODBYE

Watching them lower you in the ground,
(Motionless) I'm just standing there,
Thinking to myself " Damn that's my mans in there",
Flashing back on the good times,
Warm salty tears race from my eyes to my chin,
Who can I call when shit hits the fan now?
Who is going to stop me from shooting someone when I black out?
Nobody!
I am thankful for the time we shared, but life goes on,
It's never goodbye, I will see you again,
Until then, back to this marathon.

LETTER TO NIPSEY

I never thought I would be writing you a letter that you would never receive. I'll start off by simply saying thank you. Thank you for the music you created and left behind; it will be played until the end of time.

Your lyrics will be debated and analyzed in barbershops across the nation. Thank you for making the transition from the streets to the executive suites. Your success brought me to two realizations – 1.) anything is possible, and 2.) once you stand for something positive, the people will stand with you.

You were the peoples champ. The world loved you. You were a savior to some, and a messiah to others. You gave many people hope. You gave us inspiration when we needed it most. When the world gave up as a collective, you shifted us into positive thinking with the marathon philosophy. You reminded us to just pace ourselves and finish whatever we start.

I have so many songs of yours I like, but if I had to pick a favorite it would be "On the Floor" from your Slauson Boy 2 mix tape. Your verse spoke to my soul. The lyrics gave me chills and reassurance that one day everything will be okay. Not too many songs can do that this day and age.

Your lyrics will inspire a new leader to pick up where you left off. Maybe it's me; maybe I am the chosen one to lead the people now. I don't know, Nip. But, if I am, you left a plethora of free game behind I can use to maneuver through the traps in this world.

It's sad that you are no longer with us, but I feel good waking each day knowing you are up there watching over me as my marathon continues. Your legacy is what inspired this book. I'm anxious to see what other people will do to make you proud. You didn't die you just multiplied. You are me, now, and I am you. You planted seeds in the minds of many including myself. I took all the information and put my little twist on it. Your songs are now omens. They took you from us, but we won't let you down. The Marathon will continue!

Thanks again for the legacy you left behind. As you know, kings don't live long down here on earth, so if they get me before my message catches on, I told my family not to worry, I'm up in heaven with Nipsey. I told them to just know that I'm good and to just keep running their marathons. Rest in Peace, Nipsey. You will be forever missed!

See you when I get there,

Brother Brown

P.S.: It's a shame that you will not be able to read this book. I feel as if you passed me the torch. It's on me to continue the mission. This book will make you proud. On your last song, you instructed me what to do if you passed away.

Live my life and grow
Finish what I started
Reach them heights you know
(Lyrics from Racks in The Middle)

I'll take it from here.

Live or die,
Either or,
Go for broke,
Hustle hard,
Leave it all,
On the floor,

-Nipsey Hussle

WHEN I DIE....

And you can no longer reach me,
For an interview,
Or to catch up,
Or just to shoot the shit,
Cry for Me,
Weep for Me,
Miss me,
Keep My Name Alive,
I'm with the Lord now,
Do me a favor while you are living,
Pass my book on to the youth,
Tell them my story,
The mind is universal,
We share the same thoughts,
I went through every emotion,
I failed many times,
More than I've won actually,
People have betrayed me,
That I would have killed for,
I doubted myself most of my life,
I kept striving though,
Trying new things,
Constantly reinventing myself,
I loved hard, and was left heartbroken a few times,
Love heals all though,
In time I found love again,
Whatever you are pursuing,
Do not quit,
Get what you deserve,
If you fall short of your glory,
Read this poem again, I'm with you in spirit,
From my marathon to yours,
Pace Yourself,
You will get all that is coming to you.
- Brother Brown

If the police kill me for whatever reason they find reasonable. Please do not let them paint a negative picture of me. If they try to use my 2 mug shots to justify the demise my character, do not believe the hype. Yes, I've made mistakes but they were just things that I did; they shouldn't define my entire existence. This is my defense while I am alive. A dead man can't defend himself. The media is good at pitching a negative connotation when it comes to people of color.

*These are two mug shots of me while incarcerated on two different charges. These will be used as ammo to tarnish my character. If you are going to tell it, I just ask that you TELL IT ALL! **TELL IT ALL!**

To White America:

- I completed all your high school requirements and earned my diploma.

- I completed 4 years of college and received my Bachelor's Degree in Criminal Justice.

- I scored high enough on your ASVAB test and fought for this country on behalf of your army for 6 years.

- Everything I've done in life was in attempt to make the best of the situation.

In your eyes I am just another nigga, but I could care less about the opinion of others. I am who I am, and that is #Brother Brown.

BOOKS

These are a few books that I've enjoyed reading.

BOOK RECOMMENDATIONS

The following books are recommendations from my personal library that I've enjoyed reading:

- How to Hustle and Win Part 1&2 – Supreme Understanding.
- Knowledge of Self – Supreme Understanding.
- Letters to a young Poet – Rainer Wilke.
- Letters to a Young Brother – Hill Harper.
- The Conversation – Hill Harper.
- The Alchemist – Paulo Coelho.
- Warrior of the Light – Paulo Coelho.
- The Outsider – Colin Wilson.
- Message to the Black Man – Elijah Muhammed.
- Contagious – Jonah Berger.
- The Celestine Prophecy – James Redfield.
- The Way of the Superior Man – David Dierda.
- The Art of War – Sun Tzu.
- Pimpology – Pimpin' Ken.
- Three Magic Words – US Anderson.
- The Art of Seduction – Robert Greene.
- Pimp – Iceberg Slim.
- The Instant Millionaire – Mark Fisher.
- Contagious – Jonah Berger.
- The Secret Science – John Baines.

THE FINISH LINE

Thanks for running this marathon with me. I commend you for completing the 26 miles. Before we part pays I want to let you know that life will continue to throw blows at you. Depression and Stress will visit again. Stay strong and don't let it get the best of you. It's just a mile on the track of life. Keep running. Learn the lesson to avoid the problem next mile around. Each mile you run, each mile you reach you will build stamina and accumulate wisdom. Use that, as your GPS through life and you will avoid having to constantly reroute to reach your destination.

BEFORE YOU RUN YOUR RACE,

YOU GOT TO FIND A PACE,

JUST MAKE SURE YOU CROSS THE LINE,

FUCK THE TIME IT TAKES,

- NIPSEY HUSSLE, PERFECT TIMING

From My Marathon to Yours, Pace Yourself.

- Brother Brown

SPECIAL THANKS

I want to thank a few people that helped me on my marathon on an individual level. I wouldn't be where I am without the assistance each of you gave. Thanks to:

- Worldwide Gooch – for always having $100 for me at a moment's notice. Love you, little bro.

- Curtis – for letting me sleep on your floor and couch during them college days. Love you for grinding and staying optimistic with me bro!

- Tone – for partying with me when no one else wanted to because they had girlfriends.

- Mom – for the unconditional love and support.

- Uncle Walt – for them life talks we had riding around when I worked with you.

- Aunt Lisa – for letting me move in with you to finish high school. Thanks for letting me hold the car. Love you forever.

- Brother Sunflower – The unconditional love and understanding. We gone win in the long run.

- Chris Barr – for letting me borrow money when times was hard.

- Poop and Rick – for keeping me out of the streets and keeping me on the right path.

- John Willy – for always having a basketball league for me to play in to keep me busy year round.

- Coach G/Coach Osco – for them life talks before basketball practice every day.

Keep Running...

- Gramz - for raising me and keeping food in the pot every day.

- My Boosters - for keeping me fresh and giving me them wholesale deals.

- Police Officers - the ones that let me go when I showed them my military ID.

- Melissa - for staying down and loving me through a 2-year depression and funk. You are a true soldier with a heart of gold. Better days are coming.

- Dr. Bass - for the psychology jewels you dropped on me.

- Dr. Simon - for being a great teacher and helping me understand how this world works.

- Dr. Todd - for being anal when critiquing my college papers. It made me a better writer.

- Dr. White - for reaching out to find me employment using your contacts.

- Jamil - for the real talks we have and for keeping me sane during a rough stage in my life.

- The Huntsmen - for that free trip to Charlotte when I was broke.

- Catdaddy - for being there for me no matter the situation.

- Myra - for bringing me food when you could. I enjoyed our relationship.

- Shenise - for having a beautiful soul no matter the situation.

- Phatman - for teaching me how to hustle and sharpen my sales skills.

Keep Running...

- Mr. Richard – for the no interest loans and just being a positive person.

- Coach Spook/ Jerl – for the free cuts when I couldn't afford it.

- Chalet – for doing my math homework in college. You are the reason I graduated. Math and I don't get along.

- Frog the Barber – for the jewels you dropped on me at the Morehouse

  Barbershop.

- Alysha – for letting me stay with you behind your fathers back. Unconditional love. I was just trying my best to survive by any means.

- GG – for reading my poems and giving honest criticism.

- All my customers who support me when I am selling things.

- Soul – for showing me the ins and outs of Atlanta when I arrived on the campus of Clark Atlanta University.

- Mrs. Raglin – for keeping me aware of jobs while in undergrad.

- Cousin Coop – that one time you gave me gas money.

- Herb Moore – for the Book donation.

- Slick Rick – For the book donation.

- Meeka – for making the best macaroni ever.

- Supreme Understanding – all the jewels you dropped on me.

- Yesenia Rojas – for the book donation.

- The E4 Mafia – it was an honor to serve with you.

- Lunchy – for being an actual female best friend.

Keep Running...

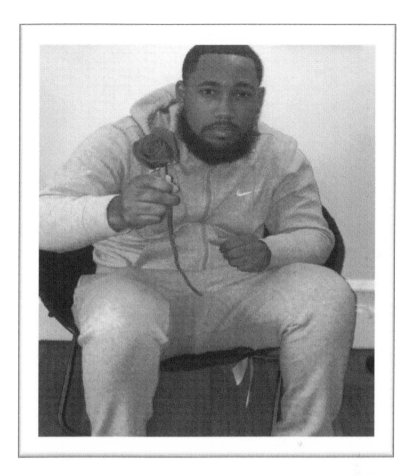

Here is your flower while you can smell it. Thank you for reading my book.

REMEMBER THIS:

"THERE ARE MANY BROWN BROTHERS, BUT THERE IS ONLY ONE BROTHER BROWN."

PACE YOURSELF,

BROTHER BROWN